THE GREAT BOOK OF PENNSYLVANIA

The Crazy History of Pennsylvania with Amazing Random Facts & Trivia

A Trivia Nerds Guide to the History of the United States Vol.8

BILL O'NEILL

ISBN: 978-1-64845-009-9

DON'T FORGET YOUR
FREE BOOKS

GET THEM FOR FREE ON
WWW.TRIVIABILL.COM

CONTENTS

CHAPTER FOUR

CHAPTER SIX
PENNSYLVANIA'S URBAN LEGENDS, UNSOLVED MYSTERIES, AND OTHER WEIRD FACTS!

INTRODUCTION

How much do you know about Pennsylvania?

Sure, you know it's located in the Northeast, but what else do you *really* know about the state? Do you know why it's called Pennsylvania? Do you know how the state earned its nickname "The Keystone State"?

By now, you've heard of Philly cheesesteaks, but do you know what other foods Pennsylvania is known for? You might know about the state's most famous chocolate company, but do you know what other popular foods were invented in PA?

You know about the Hershey chocolate factory, but do you know how it got started? Do you know how Hersheypark got started? Hint: It wasn't originally meant to be a theme park. Do you know what other amusement parks can be found in the Keystone State?

If you have ever wondered the answers to these or other questions about Pennsylvania, then you've come to the right place! This isn't just any book about PA. It's filled with interesting facts and stories about the Keystone State. Whether you live in Pennsylvania or you're thinking of planning a trip, you're bound to learn something new about the state once you've read this book.

Pennsylvania is a state that's rich in both history and culture. We'll bounce around some as we look at some of the most interesting historical facts about the Keystone State. You'll learn more about Pennsylvania's history, pop culture, attractions, inventions, and sports!

This book is broken up into six easy to follow chapters that will help you learn more about Pennsylvania. When you've finished with each chapter, you'll find a Q&A so that you can test what you've just read.

Some of the facts you'll read are surprising. Some of the facts are sad, while others may leave you with goosebumps. But one thing all of these facts have in common is that all of them are interesting. Once you've finished this book, you'll walk away with knowledge that will even impress your history teacher!

This book will answer the following questions:

How did Pennsylvania get its name?

Why is it known as the "Keystone State"?

Do you know how Hersheypark got started?

Do you know which best-selling musician had her first concert at a fair in Pennsylvania?

Which famous board game was invented by a Pennsylvanian using stolen ideas from other board games?

Which famous fast food item started out in PA?

Who was the Stroudsburg Rain Man?

What places in Pennsylvania are said to be haunted?

Where are you most likely to find Thomas Jefferson's ghost?

And so much more!

CHAPTER ONE

PENNSYLVANIA'S HISTORY AND OTHER FACTS

The state of Pennsylvania is located in the northeastern United States. The Appalachian Mountains run through the state's center. Pennsylvania is one of the original 13 colonies. How much do you know about PA? Do you know where the state got its name? How about its nickname? Do you know why Philadelphia is called "The City of Brotherly Love"? Do you know if any United States presidents have come from Pennsylvania? Read on to find out the answers to these questions and other facts about the state.

How Pennsylvania Got Its Name

Have you ever wondered where Pennsylvania's name came from? Many people say that the name came from the state's founder, William Penn. Although this is *technically* true, it was actually King

Charles II of England who gave Pennsylvania its name.

Penn was a Quaker who came to America in 1682. Since Quakers weren't well-liked in England, Penn brought other Quakers to the area with him. He established Pennsylvania as a place where people could live in the freedom of religion. People with minority religious sects from Germany, Holland, Scandinavia, and Great Britain settled into the area.

William Penn had originally been given the land by King Charles II. The land had been a payment for a debt that had been owed to Penn's deceased father Sir William Penn, who had been an English politician and admiral.

William Penn also purchased land from the Native Americans who lived west of the land he'd been given, leading to what would eventually become the state's borders.

It might surprise you to learn that Pennsylvania was not the state's first name. William Penn originally named the 40,000 square miles that he had founded "New Wales." He later called the area "Sylvania," which is the Latin word for "woods." King Charles II turned down both of these ideas, however.

In 1681, King Charles II named the area "Pennsylvania"—a combination of Penn's surname and "woods." Although William Penn was allegedly afraid that settlers would think he had named the area after himself in vanity, King Charles II hadn't actually named the area after Penn. Charles II had chosen the name in honor of William Penn's father. It's said the King had been fond of Sir William Penn, who is considered to be a historical figure of importance to the English navy.

Philadelphia Was Once America's Capital

Today, the capital of the United States is in Washington, D.C. But did you know that, prior to that, it was actually located in Pennsylvania?

Philadelphia served as the country's second capital. (New York City served as the country's first capital from 1785 to 1790). Philadelphia acted as the nation's temporary capital from 1790 to 1800 while the new permanent capital in the District of Columbia was being built.

Before Philadelphia even officially became the nation's capital, it was also where the Declaration of Independence was written. In 1776, the Second Continental Congress met at the Pennsylvania State House, which is known today as Independence Hall. It was this document that led America to form the United States of America and is what ultimately sparked the American Revolution.

After the war ended, Pennsylvania was the second

state to ratify the U.S. Constitution. (The first state was Delaware).

Philadelphia was the capital of the United States over the course of the Revolutionary War.

Philadelphia Used to be the Capital of Pennsylvania

You probably already know that the capital of Pennsylvania is Harrisburg today. It might not surprise you to learn that, like most states, Pennsylvania's capital has moved multiple times since the state was established. But do you know what other cities first served as the capital of Pennsylvania?

Before Philadelphia was the temporary capital of the nation, it first served as the capital of Pennsylvania. In fact, Philadelphia was originally founded by William Penn to serve as the capital of the Pennsylvania Colony. When it was decided that Philly would act as the temporary capital for the nation, the state capital was moved to Lancaster.

The capital was later moved to Harrisburg in 1812, where the capital remains today. President Theodore Roosevelt once called Pennsylvania's current state capital "the most beautiful state Capital in the nation."

Why PA is Known as "The Keystone State"

Have you ever wondered why Pennsylvania is nicknamed "The Keystone State"?

Well, in order to understand the nickname, it's important to first understand what a keystone is. It's a wedge in an arch that locks all of the other pieces of the arch in place. It's the most significant part of the arch—the part that all of the other parts rely on.

Pennsylvania was given the nickname "The Keystone State" because of its importance as a state. There are a few theories on why it was given its name.

For starters, there's Pennsylvania's geographic location as the middle of the original 13 colonies. It resembles a keystone—the arch that holds all of the other states in place.

However, it's also believed that the nickname holds more meaning than that. Pennsylvania has also played a key role in the political, social, and economic development of America. The state has ties to the Declaration of Independence, the U.S. Constitution, and the Gettysburg Address.

While it's not known where the state's nickname originated from or who came up with the idea, it is known that has been used since approximately 1800. When Thomas Jefferson was elected as president in 1802, Pennsylvania was called "the keystone of the federal union."

The official state song "Pennsylvania" mentions "Keystone of the land" in the second verse.

Philadelphia Was Also Home to Many Firsts

Philadelphia has impacted our country in ways you may not even know. Did you know that a number of significant "firsts" have happened in the city of Philadelphia?

Back in 1740, an academy started offering classes. This academy later became the University of Pennsylvania. While it wasn't the first university in the country, it was the first nonreligious university in the United States.

Philadelphia was also home to the country's first established hospital. Pennsylvania Hospital was established in 1751 by Benjamin Franklin and Dr. Thomas. The hospital had the first amphitheater in the United States, as well as the first medical library.

Benjamin Franklin was also responsible for founding the nation's first library, the Library Company of Philadelphia, back in 1731. It was the first lending library in the United States and helped pave the way to the first free public library.

Although the first insurance company was founded in Charleston, South Carolina back in 1732, the longest operating insurance company that's still in existence is located in Philadelphia. Philadelphia

Contributionship was formed by Benjamin Franklin in 1752.

Why Philadelphia is Known as the City of Brotherly Love

You've probably heard that Philadelphia is nicknamed "The City of Brotherly Love." Have you ever wondered where the name originated from?

It might surprise you to learn that Philadelphia's nickname is actually derived from the meaning of its name. Philadelphia, which was named by William Penn, is a combination of the Greek words "phileo" (which means "love") and "adelphos" (which means "brother"). Combined, these words mean "brotherly love."

You might be wondering why Penn chose this name meaning for the city. Penn wanted to stay on good terms with the Lenape tribe that had originally settled on the land that was to become Philadelphia. Although the land had been included in Charles II's charter as part of Penn's debt repayment, Penn decided to push it aside and bought the land directly from the Lenape tribe. Penn and a Lenape chief, who was named Tammany, ended up making a friendship treaty with one another. This is why Penn chose "brotherly love" as the city's name meaning.

This Legendary American Pioneer is From Pennsylvania

Did you know that American pioneer and legendary frontiersman Daniel Boone was born in the Keystone State?

Today, Daniel Boone is most famous for his exploration of what is known today as Kentucky. At the time, it was still a part of Virginia. Boone blazed his famous Wilderness Road from Tennessee and North Carolina through the Cumberland Gap in the Cumberland Mountains. In 1778, he founded Boonesborough, Kentucky, which was one of the very first settlements west of the Appalachian Mountains. In folklore, Boone was also famous for his hunting and trapping abilities.

But did you know that Daniel Boone's life started out in what's today known as Birdsboro, Pennsylvania? Boone spent his early years on the family's frontier, which is located near several Lenape Indian villages. The Boone family were neighbors of Mordecai Lincoln (Abraham Lincoln's great-great-grandfather). Mordecai's son Abraham actually married Daniel Boone's first cousin.

Today, you can visit the Daniel Boone Homestead in Birdsboro, PA. Spanning across 579 acres of land, the historic site is dedicated to preserving the history of both Daniel Boone and 18th century Pennsylvania settlers.

The Pennsylvania Dutch Aren't Actually Dutch

It may surprise you to learn that the Pennsylvania Dutch aren't actually Dutch as you might have always believed. They're actually German! Why is this Pennsylvania ethnic group called "Dutch" then, you ask?

When they immigrated to America, the Germans were called the Pennsylvania "Deutsch," the German word for Germanic people. The word "Deutsch" got lost in translations and eventually evolved into "Dutch" in the English language. As a result, this has led many people to believe that the Dutch are from Holland when they're really not.

Pennsylvania is Home to the Largest Amish Population in the United States

You may already know that Pennsylvania is home to the largest Amish population in the entire country. But do you know just how large it is?

As of 2018, there were 76,620 Amish people living in the state of Pennsylvania, accounting for 0.60% of the state's total population. (The state with the second-highest Amish population is Ohio, which was home to 75,830 Amish as of 2018 and the third is Indiana with 54,825 people).

Pennsylvania is also home to one of the largest Amish settlements in the United States. This settlement is located in Lancaster County, PA.

The Amish population in Pennsylvania dates back to the 18th century. It was then that the Amish first began migrating to PA from Palatinate, which is located in southwestern Germany. They migrated due to the religious wars, religious persecution, and poverty in Europe.

The Amish chose to migrate to Pennsylvania because it was known for its religious tolerance, thanks to William Penn. They were also drawn to the region due to its rich soil and mild climate. The earliest Amish originally went to Berks County, Pennsylvania, but most ended up leaving and settling in Lancaster County.

Today, most of the Amish speak "Pennsylvania Dutch" (Pennsylvania German).

Lancaster County is a major tourist attraction thanks to the Amish community, which is known for its handmade items, farmers' markets, and restaurants.

This Famous Pennsylvania Tradition Has Celtic Roots

You probably already know by now that Punxsutawney Phil of Groundhog Day fame lives in Punxsutawney, Pennsylvania. On February 2nd of every year, Phil determines how far away spring weather is. Legend says that if Phil sees his shadow and returns to his hole, there will be six more weeks of winter-like conditions. If Phil doesn't see his shadow, then spring is said to be on its way.

While Punxsutawney Phil's prediction is celebrated locally on Groundhog Day, the groundhog's prediction is aired throughout the country. The celebration has been taking place every year since 1887.

Have you ever wondered where the tradition came from? Who had the idea to let a groundhog determine whether or not spring weather was coming?

The celebration actually has Celtic roots. The tradition originated from the Pagan holiday of Imbolc (which was also known as Candlemas, among Christians). According to the Pagans, cold weather will last six more weeks if a hibernating animal casts its shadow on February 2nd. When a shadow isn't cast, spring comes early. The tradition evolved into a German belief that if the sun appeared on February 2nd, a hedgehog would cast its shadow and there would be snow until May. When Germans immigrated to Pennsylvania, they continue with their tradition with one small change: they replaced hedgehogs with groundhogs since they were indigenous to the area.

The Worst Nuclear Accident in American History Happened in Pennsylvania

Did you know that the worst nuclear accident in United States history took place in Pennsylvania? It happened in March of 1979 on Three Mile Island, which is located just south of Harrisburg, PA.

The accident happened at the Three Mile Island Nuclear Generating Station. It was caused by a series of system malfunctions, as well as human errors. The plant's nuclear reactor partially melted, leading thousands of residents to need to evacuate or flee the area due to the risk of radiation exposure.

It's believed that the accident increased cancers from 1979 to 1985 among people who lived within a 10-mile radius of Three Mile Island. That being said, researchers disagreed on how many of these cancers were caused by the nuclear accident.

Pennsylvania is the Chocolate Capital of the United States

Pennsylvania is considered the "Chocolate Capital of the USA" and for good reason. Some of the most popular chocolates in America were founded by a Pennsylvanian chocolatier.

It all started out when Milton S. Hershey was just 14 years old. After being fired from a local print shop, his mom and aunt suggested that he learn the art of candy making. His mother arranged for Hershey to do an apprenticeship with a confectioner in Lancaster, Pennsylvania.

The apprenticeship lasted for four years and by 1873, Hershey had opened his own candy shop in Philadelphia. He left the shop to do an apprenticeship with a confectioner in Denver, Colorado, who taught him to make caramel. Hershey later returned to Pennsylvania and started the Lancaster Caramel Company in 1886. In 1893, Hershey sold his caramel company for $1 million (or the equivalent of more than $29 million today) and shifted his focus to chocolate manufacturing. So, in 1896, Hershey built a milk-processing plant where he created a recipe for milk chocolate candies. By 1900, he had begun to manufacture Hershey's Milk Chocolate Bars. Three years later, Milton Hershey began building a chocolate plant in his hometown, which was then known as Derry Church. Today, the town is known as Hershey, Pennsylvania, in honor of the chocolatier.

At the time, Derry Church was a very inexpensive place to live, which drew a lot of people to the town to work for Hershey. The factory was somewhat depressing for employees, however, as Hershey had it built without windows so there wouldn't be any potential distractions. In an attempt at boosting employee morale, Hershey built an area in Derry Church where residents could enjoy leisure activities. That place is what we know today as Hersheypark.

As the chocolate bars became popular, the company began to expand rapidly. By 1907, Hershey had invented a new candy, which he named the "Hershey's Kiss." Hershey's kisses were originally wrapped by hand in their iconic aluminum foil. By 1921, a machine to wrap them was introduced. The machine also added the paper ribbon to the top of the candy to let people know it was an authentic Hershey product. Today, 80 million Hershey's Kiss candies are produced on a daily basis.

During the 1920s and 1930s, Hershey began to release a number of other chocolatey creations.

In 1925, Hershey introduced Mr. Goodbar, which contained peanuts in milk chocolate.

Hershey's Syrup came about in 1926.

Hershey's semisweet chocolate chips hit the market in 1928.

Hershey's Krackel bar, which contains crisped rice, was introduced in 1938.

Milton S. Hershey died of pneumonia in 1945. He was 88 years old at the time of his death.

In 1963, the Hershey Chocolate Corporation acquired the H.B. Reese Candy Company, which was best-known for its Reese's Peanut Butter Cups. Within six years of the acquisition, Reese's Peanut Butter Cups had become Hershey's top-selling candy.

As of 2012, Reese's was the bestselling brand of candy in the United States and the 4th bestselling brand of candy throughout the world.

In 1988, Hershey had acquired the Cadbury brand.

Today, Hershey's has plants in many locations— including plants in the cities of Lancaster and Hazleton, Pennsylvania. There are also plants located in Stuarts Draft, Virginia; Memphis, Tennessee, Robinson, Illinois, and Guadalajara, Mexico.

And to think it all started out because of one Pennsylvanian mom's suggestion!

This Pennsylvania Town Has Been on Fire Since the 1960s

Did you know that one town in Pennsylvania has been on fire for more than 50 years?

Centralia, Pennsylvania has been burning since 1962 when the coal mine caught on fire in 1962. Due to a constant supply of fuel, the fire has continued to burn ever since then.

Today, Centralia is basically a ghost town, with only seven residents who have continued to live in the town, as of 2013.

Centralia has been a tourist attraction, drawing in people who want to capture photos of the smoke and steam that can be seen throughout the borough.

One of the Worst Presidents of All-Time Came From PA

You might be surprised to learn that, in spite of Pennsylvania's rich history, only *one* United States President has ever come from that state—and he has been consistently ranked as one of the worst U.S. presidents of all-time by historians.

James Buchanan, who was the 15th President of the United States, was born in Cove Gap, Pennsylvania.

Historians often name him as one of the worst presidents in American history because he didn't address the issue of slavery. Buchanan felt that Congress shouldn't play a role in determining the slavery status of states and felt that the rights of slave-owners should be protected in any federal territory. Buchanan's decision not to address the issue has been voted as the worst presidential mistake ever made. It also brought the country to the brink of civil war, which ensured immediately after Buchanan left office.

His faults aside, Buchanan has had some unique features in comparison to other American presidents. He was the only president in the history of the United States who stayed a lifelong bachelor. Rumor has it that he may have been gay. Buchanan was also the last president who was born during the 18th century.

A Former U.S. Vice President Also Hails from the State

Did you know that former Vice President Joe Biden is from Pennsylvania? Biden was born in Scranton, PA, where he lived until the age of 10!

Biden later went on to serve as Vice President to President Barack Obama.

After Biden left office in 2017, he joined the faculty at the University of Pennsylvania.

It might also surprise you to learn that Biden wasn't the only one in his family to have held a political office. Biden's maternal great-grandfather, Edward Francis Blewit, was a former member of the Pennsylvania State Senate.

RANDOM FACTS

1. As of 2018, Pennsylvania had the 5th highest population in the United States. With 12.8 million residents, the state is only surpassed by California, Texas, Florida, and New York (in order) in terms of population. An estimated 3.91% of the United States' residents live in Pennsylvania. Pennsylvania is the 33rd largest state by area in the country. Encompassing 45,888 square miles, it's the 9th most densely populated state in the USA.

2. The two most populated cities in Pennsylvania are Philadelphia and Pittsburgh. Philadelphia is home to an estimated 1.56 million people, while approximately 303,625 people live in Pittsburgh. With an estimated 118,032 residents, Allentown has the 3rd largest population in Pennsylvania and ranks as the 231st largest city in the country. Pennsylvania's capital, Harrisburg, is the state's 10th largest city.

3. Pennsylvania is the only one of the USA's original thirteen colonies that don't border the Atlantic Ocean.

4. Pennsylvania is one of only four states in America that calls itself a commonwealth. (The other three

states are Kentucky, Massachusetts, and Virginia). It's technically called the "Commonwealth of Pennsylvania." There's no real difference between a "commonwealth" and a "state" in regards to politics or laws, however. It's just a difference in name.

5. Johnny Appleseed planted his first apple nursery just south of Warren, Pennsylvania, on Brokenstraw Creek. It's believed that his second apple nursery was planted along the shore of French Creek in Venango County, PA. According to some legends, Johnny Appleseed may have practiced his planting skills in the Wilkes-Barre, Pennsylvania area during the late 1790s, though this hasn't been confirmed.

6. Most people who live in Pennsylvania don't refer to the state by its full name. Instead, they call it simply "PA."

7. Pennsylvania is the first U.S. state to list its official website URL on its license plates.

8. A couple of historical gas stations were opened in Pennsylvania. The oldest gas station in the country is located in PA. Reighard's Gas Station, which is located in Altoona, opened back in 1909. Although it serves as a modern gas station today, it originally sold gasoline to horse and buggies when it first opened. The first drive-in gas station

in the country opened in Pittsburgh in 1913. The Gulf Station, which was a pagoda-style building with a canopy, sold gas for 27 cents per gallon when it opened.

9. Kennett Square is known as the Mushroom Capital of the World. The Pennsylvania town produces one million pounds of mushroom on an annual basis. The town is also home to a mushroom festival that takes place every year.

10. Pennsylvania was once a leading producer of oil. Back in 1881, the state was responsible for producing more than 75% of the world's oil.

11. Like other states, Pennsylvania is home to a number of strange laws. For starters, it's not legal to sleep on a refrigerator outdoors. You can't sing in the bathtub, so say goodbye to your shower karaoke sessions if you plan to move to this state. It's illegal to catch a fish with any part of your body, except for your mouth. You also can't use dynamite to catch fish. It's not legal to buy more than two packages of beer at a time unless you're purchasing from a beer distributor. Sixteen women cannot reside together in the same home since that constitutes as a brothel. Drivers who spot a team of horses coming in their direction must pull off the road, cover their vehicle with a blanket that blends in with the countryside, and allow the horses to pass. And finally, up until

2018, fireworks could not be sold to Pennsylvania residents, but it was legal for fireworks to be sold in the state.

12. Pennsylvania state slogan is "Pursue Your Happiness." The slogan was chosen in March of 2016. It was declared that happiness was the keystone of Pennsylvania.

13. The official Pennsylvania State Flag was authorized by the General Assembly in 1799. The gold-fringed banner has the Coat of Arms, which features a gold eagle resting above a boat between two black stallions, embroidered on a field of blue. The Coat of Arms lays against a blue background.

14. The Great Dane is the official state dog. William Penn even had a Great Dane. In fact, you can find a portrait of Penn and his Great Dane in the Governor's Reception Room in Harrisburg, Pennsylvania. Today, the Great Dane is a popular pet throughout the state. However, the Great Dane has a history as a popular working and hunting breed in frontier Pennsylvania. The breed was chosen as Pennsylvania's state dog back in 1965.

15. The firefly was chosen as the state insect back in 1974. However, there was some confusion about the insect's name. Most Pennsylvanians refer to

fireflies as "lightning bugs." As a result, some people in the state confused the word "firefly" with "blackfly," which was a common pest in 1988. The General Assembly rewrote the State Insect law to include the firefly's Latin name (*Poturis Pensylvanica De Geer*) so that there would be no more confusion.

16. Pennsylvania is one of only a few states in the country that has an official state locomotive. In fact, it actually has *two*: the K4s, which is the official state steam locomotive and the GGI 4859, the state electric locomotive.

17. The word "Pennsylvania" is spelled incorrectly on the Liberty Bell. This is because the bell was constructed during the days of creative spelling before the official spelling was decided on.

18. The official state animal of Pennsylvania is the white-tailed deer. While it's considered to be a pest by most residents of the state today, the white-tailed deer has played a key role in the state's early history. It provided food, clothing, and shelter to both Native Americans and the state's early settlers.

19. Pennsylvania is known for some of its humorous town names. When driving through the state, you'll spot signs for towns called Cheesetown, Jugtown, Blue Ball, Intercourse, Climax, and Big Beaver.

20. Pennsylvania has the nation's highest number of registered hunters, covered bridges, rural population, pretzel companies, and sausage production.

Test Yourself – Questions

1. Pennsylvania was named after:

   a. William Penn
   b. Sir William Penn
   c. King Charles II

2. Philadelphia is home to which of the following?

   a. The first non-religious university in the country
   b. The first gas station in the country
   c. The first amusement park in the country

3. The second capital of Pennsylvania was in:

   a. Harrisburg
   b. Lancaster
   c. Philadelphia

4. The "Pennsylvania Dutch" are actually from:

   a. Holland
   b. Scotland
   c. Germany

5. Pennsylvania's state slogan is:

   a. Pursue your dreams
   b. Pursue your passion
   c. Pursue your happiness

Answers

1. b.

2. a.

3. b.

4. c.

5. c.

CHAPTER TWO

PENNSYLVANIA'S POP CULTURE

How much do you know about Pennsylvania's pop culture? Do you know what celebrities are from the Keystone State? Do you know which movies or shows have been set and/or filmed in PA? Do you know which songs have been written about Pennsylvania? Do you know which famous, best-selling musician had her first concert *ever* at one of Pennsylvania's fairs? Do you know which famous sitcom has drawn tourists to one Pennsylvania town? To find out the answers to all of these and other questions, read on!

This Best-Selling Musician Got Her Start in Pennsylvania

Today, she's one of the world's leading musicians and, with more than 40 million albums throughout the world, is one of the best-selling artists of all-time.

But did you know that Taylor Swift was born in Reading, Pennsylvania?

The singer grew up on a Christmas tree farm. Swift attended preschool and kindergarten at the Alvernia Montessori School before later transferring to the Wyndcroft School. The Swift family later moved to Wyomissing, Pennsylvania, where Taylor went to the Wyomissing Area Junior and Senior High Schools.

By the time she was nine, Taylor Swift took an interest in musical theater. She performed in Berks Youth Theatre Academy Productions. Swift also took vocal and acting lessons in New York City. She soon began to take an interest in country music, feeling inspired by Shania Twain.

When she was 11 years old, Swift and her mom visited Nashville where they visited record labels and submitted a demo tape of her singing Dolly Parton and Dixie Chicks karaoke cover songs. Swift was rejected, however.

The following year, she learned how to play the guitar and started to learn how to write songs.

In 2003, Taylor Swift began working with Dan Dymtrow, a music manager in New York City. She modeled for Abercrombie & Fitch during their "Raising Stars" campaign. Soon after, Swift played her own songs at the RCA Records showcase where she got an artist development deal.

When Taylor Swift was 14 years old, her family relocated to Hendersonville, Tennessee so that she could be closer to Nashville.

In 2006, Taylor Swift returned to her home state where she played her first major concert at the Bloomsburg Fair!

Since then, she's gone on to produce major hits, including her country songs "Tim McGraw," "Our Song," "Love Story," "You Belong with Me," and her pop songs, "I Knew You Were Trouble," "Shake It Off," "Bad Blood," "Blank Space," and "Look What You Made Me Do." In 2017, Swift became the first artist to ever have four albums sell one million copies in the U.S. in one week.

And to think, it all started out in Reading, PA!

A Hit 90s Sitcom Was Set in Philadelphia

The show *Boy Meets World* was a beloved favorite for most '90s kids. As part of the TGIF lineup on *ABC*, the show and its characters made its way into hearts. If you've ever watched the show, then you probably know it takes place in Philadelphia, PA.

The show focuses on Cory Matthews and his family, his best friend Shawn Hunter, and his friend and later girlfriend, Topanga Lawrence.

It might break your heart a little to learn that the Matthews' house wasn't actually located in Philadelphia. The house, which went on the market for a whopping $1.595 million in 2016, was actually located in Studio City, California. The 2,500-square foot house has 2 bedrooms and 2 bathrooms.

You might also be disappointed to learn that many of the locations featured throughout the show, including John Adams High and Pennbrook University, are fictional.

Here's one silver lining: throughout the show, Cory and his dad were both huge fans of the Philadelphia Phillies. The team *does* exist.

This Cult Film Series is Set in Philadelphia

If you're a fan of the *Rocky* film series, then you may already know that the movies are primarily set in Philadelphia (though there are also scenes set in Los Angeles, such as the climactic fight between Rocky Balboa and Apollo Creed).

Rocky Balboa's neighborhood is Kensington, which is located in north Philadelphia. His apartment in the films is located at 1818 East Tusculum Street. Some of the other most notable locations in *Rocky* include Philadelphia City hall and the Italian Market.

The house featured in *Rocky II* is located at 2313 South Lambert Street in Philadelphia.

Perhaps one of the most interesting pieces of *Rocky* history is the legendary Rocky statue. The statue, which was originally located at the Art Museum in Philadelphia, was moved because it was determined to be a "movie prop" rather than "art." It was moved to the front of the Philadelphia Spectrum. The statue was later returned to the Art Museum where it was featured in *Rocky V*. The Rocky statue was returned to the Philadelphia Spectrum after movie filming was complete.

This Childhood Star is From Bethlehem, PA

Did you know that *Disney* voice actor and childhood actor Johnathan Taylor Thomas was born in Bethlehem, PA?

Taylor, who was better known as "JTT" in the 1990s, began his career in 1990 when he played the role of Kevin Brady in *The Bradys*, which was a spinoff of the iconic show *The Brady Brunch*. A year later, JTT earned his first major role as Randy Taylor in the sitcom *Home Improvement*, where he played the TV son of actor Tim Allen and actress Patricia Richardson.

In 1994, JTT earned the voice role of young Simba in the *Disney* animated film, *The Lion King*.

Taylor continued to star in *Home Improvement* throughout his teenage years but eventually left in 1998 for school.

In 2004, he earned a guest role on *8 Simple Rules for Dating My Teenage Daughter*. He also made appearances in *Smallville*.

In 2015, JTT guest-starred in the sitcom *Last Man Standing*, where he reunited onscreen with Tim Allen and Patricia Richardson.

American Bandstand Started Out in Philadelphia

Did you know that the music and dance program *American Bandstand*, which aired from 1952 to 1989, started out in Philadelphia?

The show was made famous by Dick Clark, who hosted the show from 1956 until it ended. The show featured teenagers dancing to Top 40 songs that were introduced by Clark. At least one popular musician or band would appear on the program to sing one of their singles.

Before *American Bandstand* made its nationwide debut, it first premiered on Philadelphia station WFIL-TV Channel 6 (which is today known as WPVI-TV) back in 1950. The show was originally called *Bandstand* and was hosted by Bob Horn, who had a radio show of the same name. *Bandstand* originally featured short musical films and studio guests. The show, in this format, paved the way to the music video shows that became popular during the 1980s.

Bob Horn was bored with the show's format, however. He decided to change it to a dance program, which debuted for the first time in 1952.

The show was filmed in Studio B, which was a new addition to the original 1947 building on 4548 Market Street in West Philadelphia. Bob Horn and Lee Stewart co-hosted the show until 1955. Stewart was eventually dropped as co-host.

In 1956, Bob Horn was fired from the show after he was arrested for a DUI. Horn was also allegedly involved in a prostitution ring.

The producer of the show, Tony Mammarella, acted as a host of the show until Dick Clark was hired.

In 1956, Clark pitched *Bandstand* to the ABC network, who was looking for a show to fill its 3:30 p.m. time slot. The show was renamed *American Bandstand* when it made its nationwide debut on the ABC network in December of 1957.

The show was eventually moved to Los Angeles.

American Bandstand had a major influence on American pop culture. It was one of the most popular programs of its time. It also helped increase Dick Clark's popularity.

These Famous Brothers are From Pennsylvania

Jonathan Taylor Thomas isn't the only '90s childhood actor who's from the Keystone Stone. The Lawrence brothers are, too!

The brothers—Matt, Joey, and Andy—are perhaps best-known for starring in the series, *Brotherly Love*.

In the TV series, the real-life brothers played on-screen brothers.

The brothers were originally born with the surname Mignogna, which was later to changed to Lawrence for the entire family. While Joey was born in Philadelphia, both Matt and Andy were born in Abington Township. They all attended Abington Friends School in Jenkintown, Pennsylvania.

The most famous of the three brothers is Joey. When he was just five years old, Joey sang "Give My Regards to Broadway" on *The Tonight Show Starring Johnny Carson*. Joey later went on to have guest roles in *Diff'rent Strokes* and *Silver Spoons* before earning the role of Joey Donovan in the show *Gimme a Break!*

Joey Lawrence was the voice actor of Oliver in Disney's *Oliver & Company*.

Joey later went on to play in *Run of the House* and has had guest roles in the shows *American Dreams* and *CSI: NY*.

In 2006, Joey Lawrence performed on *Dancing with the Stars*, coming in third place in the dance competition.

Lawrence's big break in the 2000s came when he starred alongside Melissa Joan Hart in the made-for-TV ABC Family film, *My Fake Fiancé*. The movie premiere saw 3.6 million viewers, making it the most-watch TV movie in 2009.

Joey Lawrence and Melissa Joan Hart starred together again, but this time in the ABC Family TV series, *Melissa & Joey*. In the show, Melissa Joan Hart's character hires Joey as a nanny to help her care for her sister's children. Both Matthew Lawrence and Andrew Lawrence had guest roles in the show.

Matt Lawrence has also played in some pretty large roles. He played Chris Hillard in the film *Mrs. Doubtfire*. Most people would probably most recognize him as Shawn Hunter's half-brother, Jack Hunter, in the TV series *Boy Meets World*. Matt Lawrence also played with Rob Schneider in the movie *The Hot Chick*, in which he starred as Rachel McAdams' love interest.

Andy Lawrence, who is the youngest of the three brothers, has seen the least success. In addition to starring alongside his brothers in *Brotherly Love*, Andy did the voice of T.J. Detweiler in the animated series *Recess*. He also played Eric in the show *Hawaii-Five-O* and has had guest roles in *CSI: NY* and *CSI: Cyber*.

This Popular Sitcom Was Set in Scranton, PA and Brought Tourists to the Region

If you're a fan of the show *The Office*, then you probably already know that it was set in Scranton, Pennsylvania. But here's something you might not know: Scranton businesses and residents donated props to *The Office* when it was filming. The show also has drawn a lot of tourists to the area.

Diehard fans of *The Office* have visited Northeast Pennsylvania to see some of the places featured in the show. In fact, *The Office* brought a lot of tourism to the Scranton area as fans flocked to learn more about the lives of their favorite characters.

Fans of the cult sitcom still visit Cooper's Seafood House, which is a restaurant that's home to a lighthouse and pirate ship, to see where Michael Scott ate on the show. The restaurant's wait staff says that fans even ask where the characters sat and what they ate and drank.

Some of the other places that were mentioned throughout the show include Lake Wallenpaupack, the Steamtown Mall, and Poor Richard's Pub.

The University of Scranton was mentioned several times on *The Office*. The school admission staff even mentions the show to try to gain interest from potential students.

You might be wondering why the writers of the show chose to set it in Scranton, rather than a larger city like Philadelphia or New York City. It's because the point of *The Office* was for it to be very real and very specific from the get-go.

If you're a fan of *The Office*, this fact may disappoint you. While John Krasinski filmed the show's opening montage in Scranton, but most of the sitcom was actually filmed in California.

This *Full House* Actor is From Pennsylvania

Did you know that one of the actors from the TV show *Full House* is from Philadelphia, Pennsylvania?

Actor/comedian Bob Saget was born in Philadelphia. While Saget lived in California for some time, he graduated from high school in Philly. It might surprise you to learn that while Saget was attending high school, he originally planned to become a physician. It was his Honors English teacher who recognized his true potential and encouraged him to become an actor instead.

Saget went on to attend Temple University's film school, where he graduated with a B.A. While he was in the program, Saget won a merit award in the Student Academy Awards for a film he created called *Through Adam's Eyes*, which was a black-and-white film about a boy who has reconstructive facial surgery.

Today he's most famous for his role as Danny Tanner in *Full House* and *Fuller House*, but it all started out in Philadelphia!

A *Mean Girls* Actress is a Pennsylvania Native

Did you know that one of the actresses from the popular movie *Mean Girls* is from Pennsylvania? Do you know who? One hint: it's *not* Regina George.

Amanda Seyfried, who played the character of Karen Smith, was born in Allentown, PA. Seyfried graduated from William Allen High School in Allentown.

Seyfried originally had plans to attend Fordham University after graduating from high school, but she chose not to attend after she scored the role of Karen, which was the actress's breakthrough role.

Seyfried's career started out in 1996 when she first began modeling. She was featured in clothing ads for Limited Too and also appeared on the covers of the *Sweet Valley High* novel series with Leighton Meester, who go on to play Blair Waldorf in the show *Gossip Girl*.

When Amanda was 17, she stopped modeling and began waitressing in a retirement community. She started training with a Broadway coach, taking voice lessons and studying opera. She took a role as an extra in the TV show *Guiding Light* and earned a larger role in *As the World Turns*. She also played in *All My Children*.

In 2003, Amanda Seyfried auditioned to play in *Mean Girls*. Although she originally auditioned for the role of Regina George (who was played by Rachel McAdams) and was considered for the role of Cady Heron (which went to Lindsay Lohan), she was ultimately cast as Karen Smith. Seyfried, Lohan, McAdams, and actress Lacey Chabert (who played Gretchen Weiners in the film) earned an MTV Movie Award for "Best On-Screen Team."

Seyfried later went on to play Kristen Bell's murdered best friend in the show *Veronica Mars.*

In 2008, she starred in the film *Mamma Mia!* (and reprised her role in *Mamma Mia! Here We Go Again* in 2018).

In 2009, Amanda Seyfried played a lead role in the movie *Jennifer's Body*, alongside then Hollywood it-girl Megan Fox.

The following year, Seyfried earned roles in two major films. She played the female lead role in the Nicholas Sparks movie *Dear John*, alongside Channing Tatum. She also played in the movie *Letters to Juliet.*

Since then, Seyfried has played in *Red Riding Hood, In Time, Gone, Lovelace, A Million Ways to Die in the West, Ted 2, Fathers and Daughters, First Reformed,* and *Gringo.*

It has been said that Amanda Seyfried can still visit the Target in her hometown without being mobbed by fans, despite her stardom and the city's pride for one of their own making her way to fame!

And So Was the Writer of the Movie!

Amanda Seyfried isn't the only actress from *Mean Girls* who's from Pennsylvania. Actress and comedian Tina Fey is from Pennsylvania, too!

Tina, whose real name is Elizabeth Stamatina Fey, was born in Upper Darby, PA.

Her parents introduced her to comedy at a young age, sneaking her into a movie theater to see *Young Frankenstein* and watching *Saturday Night Live* with her. Today, Fey is most well-known for her own appearances on *SNL*.

She attended Cardington-Stonehurst Elementary School and Beverly Hills Middle School in Upper Darby. By the time she was in middle school, Fey already knew she wanted a career in comedy. Fey went to Upper Darby High School, where she was co-editor at the school paper, *The Acorn*, for which she anonymously wrote a satirical column called *The Colonel*.

Fey went on to attend the University of Virginia, where she studied acting and playwriting. She graduated from the University of Virginia with a B.A. in drama.

Her career in comedy started when she participated in The Second City, a Chicago-based improv comedy group. Not long after, she joined *Saturday Night Live* as a writer, later becoming head writer and a performer for the show. Her big break in comedy came when she became recognized for her satirical portrayal of Sarah Palin in 2008, alongside Amy Poehler, who portrayed Hillary Clinton.

In 2004, Fey starred alongside Lindsay Lohan in the movie *Mean Girls*, in which she played high school teacher and Mathletes coach Mrs. Norbury. Tina Fey wrote the screenplay as an adaptation of the self-help book *Queen Bees and Wannabees*.

This isn't the only movie Fey played in. She later went on to land roles in the movies *Baby Mama, Date Night, Megamind, Muppets Most Wanted, Sisters*, and *Whiskey Tango Foxtrot*.

In 2006, Tina went on to create the TV series *30 Rock*, which is said to be loosely based on her time at *Saturday Night Live*.

In 2011, Fey became a New York Times Best Seller with her memoir, *Bossypants*.

She was also a co-creator of the Netflix comedy series *Unbreakable Kimmy Schmidt*.

Fey also created the Broadway adaptation of *Mean Girls*, which debuted in 2018.

And to think that it all started out in Upper Darby!

This Pop Singer and Judge of *The Voice* Was Raised in PA

Did you know that singer Christina Aguilera was raised in Pennsylvania? The singer, who was born in Staten Island, was the daughter of a U.S. Army soldier. As a result, her family moved around a lot due to his military service. Both her mother and she have claimed that her father was both physically and emotionally abusive. Christina used music as an escape.

When Aguilera was six years old, her mom divorced her father and moved the family to Rochester, Pennsylvania, near Pittsburgh. There, they lived with Christina's grandmother.

Aguilera attended Rochester Area School District in Rochester and Marshall Middle School near Wexford, PA. She also went to North Allegheny Intermediate High School for a short time. She ended up being homeschooled because she was bullied.

When she was growing up in Pennsylvania, Christina Aguilera had dreams of becoming a singer. People in her town called her the "little girl with the big voice." While she was living in PA, Aguilera performed in local talent shows and singing competitions. When she was just eight years old, she performed "I Wanna Dance with Somebody (Who Loves Me) by Whitney Houston and won her first talent show.

In 1990, Aguilera appeared on the show *Star Search*. She sang "A Sunday Kind of Love." Aguilera was eliminated during the show's semi-finals. Christina performed the same song when she appeared on KDKA-TV's *Wake Up with Larry Richert* in Pittsburgh. It wasn't her only Pittsburgh performance. Aguilera sang "The Star-Spangled Banner" during numerous sporting events, including during a Pittsburgh Penguins hockey game, a Pittsburgh Steelers football game, and a Pittsburgh Pirates baseball game. Aguilera also sang the song during the 1992 Stanley Cup Finals.

In 1991, Aguilera auditioned for *The Mickey Mouse Club*. She wasn't old enough at the time, however, and didn't appear on the show until two years later. Aguilera co-starred on the show with Britney Spears, Justin Timberlake, Ryan Gosling, and Keri Russell.

Aguilera later went on to have a number of hits, including "Genie in a Bottle," "What a Girl Wants," "Dirrty," "Beautiful," "Fighter," and "Ain't No Other Man" and her collaborations "Lady Marmalade," "Moves Like a Jagger," and "Say Something."

Aguilera has also starred in the movie *Burlesque* and has been a judge on the singing competition show, *The Voice*.

This Iconic Actor Was a Pennsylvania Native

Did you know that the legendary James "Jimmy" Stewart was from Pennsylvania?

Jimmy Stewart was considered to be the 3rd greatest male screen legend of the Golden Age of Hollywood (No. 1 and 2 were Humphrey Bogart and Cary Grant). Five of his movies have made the American Film Institute's list of the 100 best American films ever made.

Stewart was born in Indiana, Pennsylvania. His mother was a pianist. Stewart learned to play on an accordion that his father had accepted as a gift from a guest. Stewart was often playing his accordion off-stage throughout the course of his 60-year-long acting career.

Stewart went to Mercersburg Academy prep school in Pennsylvania, from which he graduated in 1928. During his time there, he was involved in an array of extracurricular activities, including football and track, yearbook club, choir, glee club, and the school's literary society.

Jimmy Stewart's first ever appearance onstage was as Buquet in the play *the Wolves* at Mercersburg Academy Prep.

Stewart later went on to attend Princeton University. There, he studied architecture. He also played the accordion and acted at the school.

When he graduated from Princeton, Stewart went to perform in the Players' productions in Cape Cod. Other performers had included Henry Fonda and Margaret Sullavan. Stewart and Fonda developed a close friendship, even becoming roommates.

Not long after, Stewart made his first debut on Broadway in *Carry Nation*. He also had a few lines in *Goodbye Again*.

Stewart later went on to star in a number of movies, including *The Philadelphia Story*, which he won an Academy Award for. Stewart's most well-known movie, however, is *It's a Wonderful Life*.

Even to this day, the town of Indiana, Pennsylvania honors its most famous native. Each Christmas season, the downtown area of the town is decorated in the theme of *It's a Wonderful Life*.

Pretty Little Liars Was Set in Pennsylvania and is Loosely Based on the Author's Life

If you've seen the show *Pretty Little Liars*, you probably already know that the young adult thriller/mystery TV series was set in the suburbs of Philadelphia.

What you might *not* know is that the show, which was based on the book series of the same name by author Sara Shepard, is actually loosely based on the author's life.

Sara Shepard grew up in Downingtown, Pennsylvania. She graduated from Downingtown High School and later attended New York University and Brooklyn College.

Alloy Entertainment came up with the concept of *Pretty Little Liars*. They wanted to create something like *Desperate Housewives* for teenagers. They gave Sara Shepard the property to develop into a book series, with plans of producing it into a TV series.

Shepard's first book was published by HarperTeen in 2006. Two years later, Alloy announced that a TV show adaptation was in the works.

Even though the idea wasn't entirely her own, Shepard did include aspects of her own life in the series.

For starters, Shepard named one of the main characters, Alison DeLaurentis, after her own real-life sister, Alison.

Shepard has said that the fictional town of Rosewood in *Pretty Little Liars* was inspired by her own hometown.

Shepard said that she didn't have a stalker like the characters in her book series, but she did deal with some of the same issues that the characters faced—including shoplifting, confusions about sexuality, and a friend's father having an affair with a student.

Sara Shepard currently lives in Pittsburgh, PA.

The author had a cameo appearance in two episodes of *Pretty Little Liars*: "The Homecoming Hangover" and "I'm a Good Girl, I Am."

Rosewood isn't the only town or place mentioned in the book or TV series. Philadelphia and the Poconos are both featured in both the book series and the TV series. Allentown, which is said to be Caleb's hometown, is also mentioned in the TV adaptation of the series.

As for where the show was filmed? Sorry to disappoint you, but the show was actually filmed at the Warner Bros. studio and backlot in Los Angeles— *not* in Pennsylvania.

This Famous Singer/Actor is from PA

Today, he's most well-known for playing on the popular 90s sitcom *The Fresh Prince of Bel-Air* and for his song "Miami." Since then, he's gone on to play in a number of roles, including as Mohammed Ali in the film *Ali*, as well as the lead role in the movie *The Pursuit of Happyness.* Did you know that singer/actor Will Smith was born in the Keystone State?

Will, whose real name is Willard, was born in Philadelphia. He was raised in the Wynnefield neighborhood of West Philadelphia. Will went to Our Lady of Lourdes, which is a private Catholic elementary school in Philadelphia. He later attended Overbrook High School in Philadelphia.

Although he considered attending MIT for engineering, Smith never applied to college because it was his dream to become a rapper.

During the late 1980s, Smith had some fame as a rapper. He rapped under the name The Fresh Prince, which later became the basis of the title of *The Fresh Prince of Bel-Air.*

The rest is history—and it all started out in Pennsylvania!

One of the Biggest Musical Festivals in the Country Takes Place in Pennsylvania

Did you know that one of the biggest music festivals in America takes place in Bethlehem, PA?

Musikfest has been held in the city every year since 1984 and first took place in 1741. The music festival claims to be "the largest non-gated free musical festival" in the United States. The festival starts on the first Friday in August and lasts for 10 days.

The festival typically draws in more than one million visitors each year.

Musikfest is held at the Steel Stage, which is owned by Sands Casino Resort in Bethlehem. A different musician performs each night of the festival. These concerts aren't free.

Some of the most famous musicians who have performed at Musikfest over the years include Carrie Underwood, The Beach Boys, Alice Cooper, Maroon 5, George Thorogood, Carlos Santa, Duran Duran, Staind, Dixie Chicks, Ray Charles, Boyz II Men, Tony Bennett, Boston, Alice in Chains, Lynyrd Skynyrd, Martina McBride, and Live, to name a few.

In addition to the concerts, there's food and other attractions. Much of the festival incorporates the area's local German roots, but there's a celebration of a variety of ethnicities.

RANDOM FACTS

1. Singer/actress Sabrina Carpenter, who played Cory and Topanga's daughter's best friend Maya in the show *Girl Meets World*, is from PA! The actress was born in Lehigh Valley, Pennsylvania. The singer/actress got her big break when she placed 3rd in Miley Cyrus's singing contest "The Next Miley Cyrus Project." Carpenter is also known for her hit song "Thumbs."

2. *Transformers: Revenge of the Fallen*, the second installment in the movie series starring Shia LaBeouf, was filmed throughout Pennsylvania. Some of the locations you may recognize throughout Philadelphia include the University of Pennsylvania, Laurel Hill Cemetery, Delaware Power Plant, Eastern State Penitentiary, Chancellor Street, City Hall, Girard College, and the Italian Market's Cappuccio's Meats. The opening scene of the movie was filmed at the former Bethlehem Steel plant (which is now the property of Sands Casino Resort).

3. Most of the movie *Blue Valentine*, starring Ryan Gosling and Michelle Williams, was filmed in Scranton. The movie's iconic Star Gazer Fantasy Suite hotel scenes were filmed at the Radisson

Valley Forge in King of Prussia, where you can spend the night at one of the hotel's 15 fantasy suites.

4. The biographical movie *Girl, Interrupted,* starring Winona Ryder and Angelina Jolie, was filmed throughout Pennsylvania. An abandoned building in Harrisburg was used for the mental institution, which is where the majority of the movie is set. There were also scenes filmed in Lancaster, including on Pine Street near Franklin & Marshall College.

5. Actress Sharon Stone was born in Meadville, Pennsylvania. She graduated from Saegertown High School and later attended the Edinboro University of Pennsylvania. While attending the university, she won the title of Miss Crawford County, Pennsylvania and was considered a candidate for Miss Pennsylvania. She quit college to become a fashion model in New York City. In 2016, Stone completed her degree at Edinboro University, which the actress credits Hillary Clinton for inspiring her to do. Stone is most well-known for starring in the films *Basic Instinct* and *Casino.*

6. Actor Jesse Williams, who plays Dr. Jackson Avery on the show *Grey's Anatomy,* graduated from Temple University in Pennsylvania, where he majored in African-American Studies and

Film and Media Arts. Prior to taking on his role on *Grey's Anatomy*, Williams taught high school American Studies, African Studies, and English in the Philadelphia public school system.

7. Late musician Jim Croce is from Upper Darby, Pennsylvania, which is located just outside of Philadelphia. Best known for his songs "Time in a Bottle" and "Bad, Bad Leroy Brown", Croce attended Upper Darby High School, which he graduated from in 1960. He later went to Malvern Preparatory School before attending Villanova University, where he graduated with a bachelor's degree in psychology. While he was attending Villanova, he was a member of the Villanova Singer and the Villanova Spires, which performed off-campus and recorded under the name "The Coventry Lads." Croce was a student disc jockey at WKVU.

8. The movie *Marley & Me*, starring Owen Wilson and Jennifer Aniston, has scenes that were filmed in Pennsylvania. The house where their characters settle down was located in Chadds Ford, PA. The movie also features scenes that were filmed at Broad and Walnut streets in Philadelphia.

9. Singer Vanessa Carlton was born in Milford, Pennsylvania. Carlton is best known for her songs "A Thousand Miles" and "Ordinary Day."

Carlton made Pennsylvania news headlines a few years ago following a Pitbull attack while she was running in her family's neighborhood in Milford.

10. Hip-hop artist Cassidy is from Philadelphia, PA. He started his career as a freestyle and battle rapper before scoring a record deal back in 2002. Cassidy is most well-known for his songs "Hotel," "I'm a Hustla," and "My Drink n My 2 Step."

11. Singer Daya is from Mt. Lebanon, Pennsylvania. Her song "Hide Away" reached No. 23 on the *Billboard* Hot 100. She's also known for her song "New."

12. Rapper Eve is from Philadelphia, PA. In 2002, she won a Grammy Award for Best Rap/Sung Collaboration in 2002, for "Let Me Blow Ya Mind" featuring Gwen Stefani.

13. The late teen heartthrob Frankie Avalon was from Philadelphia. Once considered a teen idol, Avalon played with Bobby Rydell in Rocco and the Saints. Avalon also starred as "Smitty" in the movie *The Alamo*, alongside John Wayne.

14. Rock 'n roll singer Chubby Checker (Ernest Evans) was raised in the projects of South Philadelphia. By the age of eight, Evans had formed a street-corner harmony group. He later

took piano lessons at Settlement Music School. Evans entertained his classmates by imitating musicians of that time, including Elvis Presley and Jerry Lee Lewis. When he was attending South Philadelphia High School, Chubby Checker was classmates and close friends with Fabiano Forte, who later went on to become popular performer Fabian. Chubby Checker is most well-known for popularizing dance styles, including the twist (with his cover song "The Twist," originally by Hank Ballard) and the Pony with his hit "Pony Time."

15. Singer Anthony Green is from Doylestown, PA. In addition to having a solo career, he is the lead singer of the bands Circa Survive and Saosin.

16. Several songs have been written about the Keystone Stone. Some of these include "Allentown" by Billy Joel, "Streets of Philadelphia" by Bruce Springsteen, "You've Got a Friend in Pennsylvania" by New Found Glory, and "Philadelphia Freedom" by Elton John.

17. The late musician Lisa Lopes—who was better known by her stage name "Left Eye"—was a hip-hop singer/rapped, who belonged to the girl group TLC with Tionne "T-Boz" Watkins and Rozonda "Chilli" Thomas. Lopes was born in Philadelphia, PA and attended the Philadelphia High School for Girls. Her father was also a

musician who played the piano, harmonica, clarinet, and saxophone. Lopes started playing with a toy keyboard when she was just five years old and began writing her own songs as she got older. When she was 10, she formed a musical trio with her siblings called The Lopes Kids. They performed gospel songs at local churches and events. She later went on to be a part of TLC and is often recognized as one of the most influential members of the group. She designed the outfits and staging for the group, as well as contributing to their album titles, music videos, and more. Her nickname "Left Eye" came about because a guy once told her he found her attractive due to her left eye. She wore a pair of glasses with the left lens covered by a condom when TLC was promoting safe sex. Left Eye was also known to wear a black stripe under her left eye and also got her left eyebrow pierced. The group was most well-known for their songs "Waterfalls", "Creep", "Unpretty", and "No Scrubs." In 2002, Lisa Lopes was killed in a car accident.

18. Singer/actress Patti LaBelle was born in the Eastwick section of Southwest Philadelphia, PA. In the 1960s, she formed the vocal group, Patti LaBelle and the Bluebelles. Under their second name, Labelle, the group released the song "Lady Marmalade" and rose to success. They became

the first African-American vocal group to ever appear on the cover of *Rolling Stone* magazine.

19. Singer Pat Monahan was born in Erie, Pennsylvania. His father, who owned a clothing store, was also a musician. Pat Monahan went to McDowell High School and later attended the Edinboro University of Pennsylvania. He's most well-known as the lead singer and founding member of the band Train.

20. Louisa May Alcott, who was the author of the 1868 novel *Little Women*, was from Pennsylvania. Alcott was born in Germantown, which is now a part of Philadelphia. Alcott didn't live there for very long, however. Two years after Alcott was born, her family moved to Concord, Massachusetts.

Test Yourself – Questions

1. Taylor Swift's first concert was at:

    a. The Kutztown Fair
    b. The Allentown Fair
    c. The Bloomsburg Fair

2. Which '90s show is set in Pennsylvania?

    a. *Boy Meets World*
    b. *Full House*
    c. *Step by Step*

3. Which *Mean Girls* actress is not from Pennsylvania?

    a. Amanda Seyfried
    b. Rachel McAdams
    c. Tina Fey

4. *Grey's Anatomy* star Jesse Williams graduated from which Pennsylvania college?

    a. Temple University
    b. The University of Pennsylvania
    c. Penn State University

5. The fictional town of Rosewood in *Pretty Little Liars* is based on which Pennsylvania town?

    a. Scranton
    b. Downingtown
    c. Reading

Answers

1. c.
2. a.
3. b.
4. a.
5. b.

CHAPTER THREE

PENNSYLVANIA'S INVENTIONS, IDEAS, AND MORE

Have you ever wondered what inventions have come out of the state of Pennsylvania? Like many other states, a number of products and foods that you see in your day-to-day life have originated from the Keystone State. Did you know which famous toy came out of the state? Do you know which popular fair ride was first constructed in Pennsylvania? Do you know board game was invented by a Pennsylvanian? Do you know which popular junk foods have come out of PA? To find out more about Pennsylvania's inventions, ideas, and more, read on!

The Movie Theater

Today, they're often criticized for being an overpriced place to watch a movie and let's not even get started on the price of snacks. Did you know that the movie theater got its start in Pennsylvania?

Back in June of 1905, two Pittsburgh natives—John P. Harris and Harry Davis—opened a theater on Smithfield Street in downtown Pittsburgh. They called it the Nickelodeon. They aired *The Great Train Robbery*, which was a 10-minute film starring George Barnes. The Nickelodeon charged people five cents to view the film.

The theater, which housed about 100 chairs and a piano facing a famed screen, was a hit. Just a few months later, there were over a dozen theaters in Pittsburgh alone. Two years later, there were thousands of theaters throughout the entire country.

Today, you can find a plaque on Smithfield Street in honor of the first Nickelodeon. Though, it's worth noting that the plaque isn't entirely accurate. It states that the title of one of the first films the theater aired was *The Battled Burglar*, when, in fact, it's *The Baffled Burglar*.

The Slinky

Chances are, you've probably owned a Slinky at some point in your lifetime. Did you know that the toy that can walk downstairs was invented in Pennsylvania?

The Slinky was invented by a mechanical engineer named Richard T. James. The idea allegedly came about when James was working on springs to help the Navy balance ships during storms. He noticed how the springs rocked back and forth and thought that it could be turned into a toy.

James' invention was a success. The Slinky made its debut premiere in a Philadelphia Gimbels department store back in 1945. Since then, more than 350 million Slinkys have been purchased.

Today, the toy is produced in Hollidaysburg, Pennsylvania.

Bubble Gum

Did you know we can thank a Pennsylvanian for bubble gum?

Not to be confused with *chewing* gum (which actually dates back to the ancient Greeks), bubble gum was first invented by a Philadelphia accountant by the name of Walter Diemer. Diemer is said to have stumbled on the invention by accident.

Back in the 1920s, Diemer was working at the Fleer Chewing Gum Company where he was working on inventing a less sticky chewing gum. He allegedly invented a much stretchier form of regular chewing gum on accident. He was able to blow bubbles with the gum, but there was just one problem: the following day, he couldn't produce the same results. It took him four more months to perfect his invention. Diemer taught the entire staff at Fleer Chewing Gum Company how to blow bubbles with the gum so that customers would take notice when they came in to buy gum.

Diemer's invention came to be known as Dubble Bubble, the same bubble gum you've probably blown bubbles with yourself!

Philly Cheesesteaks

Of all its food, Pennsylvania is probably most well-known for its Philly Cheesesteaks. The traditional version of the sandwich is a combination of chopped beefsteak, onions, and melted cheese on a hoagie roll. Many restaurants also serve Philly Cheesesteaks with a variety of other vegetables, including grilled peppers and mushrooms.

Philadelphia natives Pat and Harry Olivieri were the inventors of the Philly Cheesesteak. It's been said that Pat and Harry were co-owners of a hot dog stand near the Italian Market in Philadelphia. They had the idea of a new sandwich that consisted of chipped beef and grilled onions, which they made for themselves. As Pat was eating the sandwich, a cab driver requested one. At the cab driver's suggestion, they began selling the sandwiches.

Their sandwiches were such a hit that Pat started his own restaurant in 1930. The restaurant, Pat's King of Steaks, is still open to this day.

It might surprise you to learn that the original Philly Cheesesteak sandwich didn't have cheese. A manager named Joe "Cocky Joe" Lorenza was the first to add provolone cheese to the sandwich.

Cheesesteaks are commonly found on Philadelphia restaurant menus and are a popular food cart item throughout the city. The sandwich is commonly served with fries or cheese fries.

While "Philly Cheesesteaks" can also be found at restaurants throughout most of Pennsylvania, it's often said that you haven't really had a Cheesesteak until you've had one in Philly!

The Banana Split

Did you know that the Banana Split was invented in the Keystone State?

The popular ice cream sundae was invented by a 23-year-old apprentice pharmacist by the name of David Evans Strickler. Strickler worked at Tassel Pharmacy in Latrobe, Pennsylvania, where he liked to invent sundaes at the store's soda fountain.

Strickler invented the Banana Split in 1904, which he sold for 10 cents, which was double the cost of other sundaes sold by the store. The sundae first became popular with students who were attending nearby Saint Vincent College. Soon, the sundae became so popular that it began to spread outside of Latrobe,

PA, with many ice cream stands and restaurants offering Strickler's invention.

In 1907, a popular recipe was printed for the Banana Split. It called for a banana split lengthwise, two ice cream scoops at each end topped with whipped cream, one covered with chopped mixed fruits and the other covered with chopped mixed nuts, and a maraschino cherry on top.

The annual Great American Banana Split Celebration takes place in Latrobe, PA each August. In 2004, the city celebrated the 100th anniversary of the banana split's invention. The National Ice Cream Retailers Association also named the city the banana split's birthplace.

The Arnold Palmer

The Arnold Palmer is a non-alcoholic drink that's made from 50% iced tea and 50% lemonade. The drink was invented and made popular by the golfer. It's also sometimes referred to as a "half and half" due to its equal parts of iced tea and lemonade.

The alcoholic version, which is generally made with vodka, used to be known as a John Daly. In 2018, however, MillerCoors began to sell a premade version of the drink that contains vodka, which is called "Arnold Palmer Spiked."

Although many believe that the drink was invented at Palmer's request by a country club bartender in

Palm Springs, California, Arnold Palmer himself once said that he actually invented the iced tea/lemonade combination when he was living in his hometown, Latrobe, Pennsylvania. He was said to drink the concoction both at home and at Pennsylvania country clubs.

The drink gained popularity after a woman overheard the legendary golfer ordering the drink at a bar during the 1960 U.S. Open at the Cherry Hills Country Club in Denver, Colorado. The woman ordered the same drink and the Arnold Palmer was born!

The Monopoly Boardgame

There's no doubt that Monopoly is one of the most popular board games in America. Did you know that the game traces its roots back to Pennsylvania?

The Monopoly game, which focuses on acquiring fictional real estate on a game board, was designed and named by Charles Darrow. Well… *sort of*.

You see, the idea for the game actually originated from The Landlord's Game, which had been created by Elizabeth Magie a few years earlier. It was commonly played by college professors and their students. There was another variant of the game, which was called The Fascinating Game of Finance, that was popular in the Midwest during the late 1920s/early 1930s. The game eventually made its way to the east, gaining popularity in Pennsylvania and in Atlantic City. A man named Charles Todd taught Charles Darrow how to play the game. In that version of the game, it had been customized with Atlantic City street and property names.

Charles Darrow (along with his wife and son) made their original game boards on oilcloth. Darrow drew the designs of the properties. His wife and son colored in the spaces and made the title deed cards. On his original game boards, Darrow also designed some of the game's icons that led to Monopoly's fame.

By 1934, Darrow had the game printed on cardboard. He sold copies of the game to Wanamaker's Department Store in Philadelphia.

The game was rejected by Milton Bradley and, at first, Parker Brothers. Parker Brothers changed its mind when Darrow began to get orders from other department stores.

In 1935, Darrow sold the game to Parker Brothers. Within a year, the game was selling 20,000 copies *a week*. This made it the best-selling game board that year. Charles Darrow also became the first game designer to ever become a millionaire.

Although Charles Darrow was named the sole inventor of the game, research has since found that his design was eerily similar to both The Landlord's

Game and The Fascinating Game of Finance (which were also oddly close to one another in concept and design). In fact, Darrow even used the same misspelling in his game as the one Charles Todd had taught him. Many considered Charles Darrow to be a plagiarist of the game. Even so, Hasbro still lists only him as the only inventor of Monopoly.

After Charles Darrow died in 1967 in Bucks County, Atlantic City placed a plaque in his honor on The Boardwalk.

Tastykake

Today, Tastykake is most well-known for its Kandy Kakes, Sweetie Kakes, and mini donuts. Have you ever wondered who to blame for the temptation when you see those delicious prepackaged baked snacks at the grocery store?

The credit goes to Philip J. Baur and Herbert T. Morris, who founded the company in the Germantown neighborhood of Philadelphia. They had previously owned a bakery in the Pittsburgh area, which they sold to the Ward Baking Company in 1913 under the agreement that they couldn't open another bakery within 100 miles of Pittsburgh. So, the partners moved to Philadelphia. Herbert T. Morris's wife came up with the name "Tastykake."

In 1927, Tastykake introduced its popular Butterscotch Krimpet. Not long after, the company also released individually wrapped fruit and cream pies. What we know as the Kandy Kake today was first called the Tandy-Kake when it was put out on the market in 1931.

The Tasty Baking Company quickly saw success throughout Philadelphia. The company sold $28 worth of cakes during their first day of sales at 10 cents each. By the end of 1914, they had made $300,000 in sales (or the equivalent of approximately $7.3 million today).

Since the company distributed its products using horse-drawn wagons until 1941, most of the company's sales were in Philadelphia. During World War II, the company sent thousands of cakes and pies to soldiers overseas, which helped it increase its popularity. As the company began to use trucks, electric cars, rails, and ships to increase distribution, it began to sell its products in Western PA, Virginia, and New York.

The company's sales doubled during the late 1950s and early 1960s, thanks to new machinery that helped cut the baking process from 12 hours to 45 minutes.

By 1960, the company had earned nearly $22.9 million.

The Kandy Kake is the most popular cake in the history of Tastykake. Today, nearly half a million of the cakes are baked and packaged on a daily basis.

During the 1970s and 1980s, Tastykake added new products to its line of products, including pastries, muffins, and chocolate-covered pastries.

These Types of Soda

Although carbonated drinks have been around since the mid-1700s due to the alleged health benefits, a druggist named Townsend Speakman in Philadelphia was the first to add fruit flavoring to soda water. He sold the drink as "Nephite Julep" back in 1807. His reason for adding the fruit flavoring was because people didn't like the taste of carbonated water, but they wanted to drink it for its health benefits. Nephite Julep is said to be the first "soda pop" on record.

Commercial root beer also originated from Pennsylvania. Although sassafras-flavored drinks have been around since the early 1800s, a pharmacist named Charles Elmer Hires from Philadelphia was the first who had the idea to sell it back in 1875. Hires began selling his sassafras-based "root tea" out of the store he worked at on Sixth and Spruce. A year later, he decided to market it as "root beer" and it saw much more success.

The brand Pennsylvania Dutch Birch Beer also originated from the state (and it's one of the only places where you can find it). The company's birch beer is based on a Pennsylvania Dutch recipe and has been around since 1936. Although it was previously made in Allentown and Williamsport, PA, Pennsylvania Dutch Birch Beer is produced in Pennsauken, NJ today.

The A-Treat Bottling Company is located in Allentown, PA. Though the company temporarily stopped production in 2015, it was later revived by Jaindl Companies. Some of A-Treat's most popular soda and soda pop products include Cream Soda, Black Cherry soda, Blue Razz soda, Grapefruit soda, Orange soda, Birch Beer draft soda, Root Beer Draft soda, and Pineapple soda.

Potato Chips

Okay, so potato chips weren't actually invented in Pennsylvania. They were invented by George Crum, a chef at the Moon Lake Lodge Resort in Saratoga Springs, New York.

That being said, the state of Pennsylvania *is* famous for its potato chip production. With two major potato chip companies in the state, Pennsylvania is considered to be one of the potato chip capitals of America.

The Herr's brand of potato chips was started by James S. Herr, who was only 21-years-old at the time. He bought a small potato chip company that was located in Lancaster, Pennsylvania in 1946. Sales for the company started at about $30 per week. By 1958, the company released flavored potato chips. In 1974, it switched to the foil packaging the company is known for today.

Barbecue flavored potato chips are one of Pennsylvania's inventions. Herr's was the first company to ever create barbecue-flavored potato chips, which it introduced to the market during the 1950s.

The Utz potato chips brand started out in 1921 in Hanover, PA. It was originally called "Hanover Home Brand Potato Chips." The company was established by William and Salie Utz, who began a small potato chip business out of their house. They had hand-operated equipment that allowed them to produce about 50 pounds of potato chips an hour. Salie would make the chips and Bill would later deliver them to local stores and farmers' markets in Hanover, as well as Baltimore, Maryland.

As the company grew more and more successful, the couple began operating from a small concrete building in their backyard. By 1938, they invested in equipment that allowed them to make 300 pounds of chips an hour. It wasn't until 1949 that they were able to move operations to a facility in Hanover.

By 2004, the Utz company was seeing $235 million annually, with pretzels accounting for about 10% of their sales.

Though Salie and William have both since passed, the Utz company remains family-owned.

Utz's distribution area remains on the East Coast, with sales spanning only from Maine to Florida. Still, many Pennsylvanians consider Utz chips to be the best chips.

The Ferris Wheel

Today, they can be found at fairs, carnivals, and boardwalks throughout the United States, but did you know that the very first Ferris wheel in the world was designed and built by a Pennsylvanian? Fun fact: the Ferris wheel was also named after its Pennsylvanian inventor.

The original Ferris Wheel was designed by George Washington Gale Ferris Jr., who was a bridge builder. Ferris started out his career in the railroad industry and started G.W.G. Ferris & Co. in Pittsburgh, PA, which did inspections for metals used to construct railroads and bridges. Ferris was living in Pittsburgh when he designed the wheel back in 1893.

The invention came about when the World's Columbian Exposition (a fair in Chicago, Illinois) came up with a challenge for American engineers. They wanted a monument for the fair that would be more impressive than the Eiffel Tower, which would be presented at the 1889 Paris International Exposition.

The planning commission hoped that the admissions from the monument would help eliminate the fair's debt and make it profitable over time.

When Ferris first presented his invention, the fair's planners didn't believe that the rotating wheel could be safe.

Ferris didn't give up on the idea, however. A few weeks later, he came back with endorsements from well-known engineers proposing the safety of his design, as well as $400,000 from investors. Needless to say, Ferris managed to convince the committee.

George Washington Gale Ferris Jr.'s invention stood 264 feet tall, making it the tallest attraction at the fair when it opened in June of 1893. The Ferris Wheel had 36 cars with 40 revolving chairs. It was able to accommodate up to 60 people at a time.

When the attraction first opened at the fair, the Ferris Wheel saw 38,000 daily passengers, who paid 50 cents to ride it. Before the original Ferris Wheel was demolished in 1906, it had been ridden by 2.5 million passengers.

It might surprise you to learn that Ferris didn't get rich from his invention. In fact, when the fair closed, Ferris claimed that the fair had robbed him and his investors of the money they had invested in it. He spent the rest of his life dealing with lawsuits against them.

Pretzels

Pretzels weren't actually invented in Pennsylvania. The invention dates back to 610 A.D. in Italy when they were called pretiolas or "little rewards." They were called this because Italian monks allegedly used pretzels as rewards to encourage their students to study harder.

The invention later became popular throughout Austria and Germany where they became known as "bretzels." So, of course, when the German settlers moved to Pennsylvania, they brought the invention with them.

According to legend, the first American soft pretzel was baked in Lititz, Pennsylvania back in 1861. It's been said that a baker by the name of Ambrose Roth was given the recipe by a homeless man after he provided him with shelter for the night. Roth's apprentice, Julius Sturgis, allegedly loved the recipe and donated a few hundred pretzels to Northern soldiers during the Civil War. This helped popularize pretzels.

Today, Pennsylvania is the world's leading producer of both hard and soft pretzels. Philadelphia is undeniably famous for its soft pretzels, most of which are produced in the city. Federal Pretzel Baking Company and the Center City Pretzel Company are two famous soft pretzel factories in Philly. Most pretzels today are cut by machines, but Reading Terminal Market is famous for its hand-twisted pretzels.

The two leading hard pretzel companies were also founded in Pennsylvania. Snyder's of Hanover, which is the No.1 pretzel brand is America, was started in Hanover back in 1909. The Rold Gold pretzel company was founded in Philadelphia in 1917.

The Auntie Anne's soft pretzel chain also started out in PA. The chain originally started out as a stand in 1988 at the Downingtown, Pennsylvania Farmer's Market. Today, the chain has more than 1,500 locations worldwide, which include malls, Walmart stores, amusement parks, airports, and more.

The Big Mac

Today, it's by far one of the most popular fast food items throughout the country. Did you know that McDonald's Big Mac hamburger was created in the Keystone State?

Jim Delligatti, a franchisee who owned several McDonald's restaurants in the Pittsburgh area, who created the sandwich. It was at his first franchise, which is located on McKnight Road in Ross Township, that he created the sandwich. Delligatti came up with the sandwich to compete with Eat'n

Park (a Big Boy Restaurants franchise), which had put out the Big Boy hamburger.

The sandwich was first sold in Delligatti's Uniontown, Pennsylvania McDonald's restaurant for the first time in 1967. It cost 45 cents at the time.

The Big Mac wasn't always called the Big Mac, either. Two other names were tested for the sandwich. The first was the Aristocrat, which costumers found hard to pronounce. The second was the Blue Ribbon Burger, which also turned out to be a huge failure.

The "Big Mac" stuck and the sandwich turned out to be so popular that in 1968—just one year after the sandwich's invention—it was added to all of McDonald's menus.

Today, the Big Mac isn't only popular in America. It's known throughout the entire world.

So, what makes the Big Mac different from other fast food hamburgers? It consists of two beef patties, American cheese, pickles, onions, iceberg lettuce, and the most famous aspect of the sandwich: its "special sauce" (which is a type of Thousand Island dressing).

And it all started out in the Keystone State!

Scrapple

Aside from Philly cheesesteak, Pennsylvania is most famous for scrapple. Although it can be found in a few select U.S. states in the Northeast, such as New

Jersey and Delaware, Pennsylvania is said to have the best scrapple.

A popular joke is that scrapple is made of "everything but the oink." Scrapple is a mush that's made of pork scraps, which generally includes the heart, head, liver, and other trimmings. These ingredients are boiled with any bones that are still attached (generally the entire head) to form a broth. The bones and fat are then removed. The meat is removed from the pot and cornmeal is boiled into the broth, which forms a mush. The meat is re-added to the pot and seasonings are added. The mush is then formed into a loaf and cooled. The loaf is cut into slices, which are fried in a pan prior to serving.

Traditionally, the method of cooking was used to avoid wasting scraps of meat that were leftover after butchering. Scrapple originated from pre-Roman Europe and later from Germany with a dish known as "panhas" in German. Still sometimes referred to as "panhas" (or "Pannhaas"), the German term translates to "pan rabbit" because it was traditionally made with rabbit. When the Pennsylvania Dutch settlers brought the culinary tradition to Pennsylvania with them, the recipe was adapted to use pork, which was more readily available in the region. Early German settlers in the Philadelphia region created the first American scrapple recipes during the 17th and 18th centuries.

Today, scrapple is considered to be a Pennsylvania Dutch food. It can be found at many Amish restaurants in PA, as well as supermarkets in both fresh and frozen forms. It can also be found at many diners and restaurants throughout the state.

Candy Corn

You probably either love or hate this Halloween candy, but did you know that candy corn got its start in Pennsylvania?

It was created by a Philadelphia candy maker named George Renninger of the Wunderle Candy Company during the 1880s. First known as "Chicken Feed," the candy originally only caught on with farmers in the region. The Goelitz Confectionary Company later went on to mass produce the candy. (Back in 2000, the Goelitz Confectionary Company was renamed the Jelly Belly Company).

The candy was mass-produced using sugar, fondant, marshmallow cream, corn syrup, and vanilla flavor. Although the original recipe is still used, you can now find different varieties of candy corn, including red and green for Christmas and pastel colors for Easter.

It has been estimated that approximately 35 million pounds of candy corn are sold every year.

Although candy corn is a staple of the fall season, it's

often a subject of wide debate. Much like pineapple pizza, people tend to either love or hate the candy's flavor.

RANDOM FACTS

1. Marshmallow Peeps were founded in Bethlehem, Pennsylvania by the Rodda Candy Company. In 1953, the company was acquired by a Russian immigrant named Sam Born. This would lead to Born's company, Just Born. The name "Just Born" came as a play on Sam Born's last name. He also would line up his freshly made candy chicks for sale and labeled them "just born." By the 1960s, Just Born was the leading producer of marshmallow candies. Love them or hate them, the yellow, pink, purple, and blue chicks and bunnies are an Easter staple. Today, the candies also come in seasonal colors and different flavors—and it all started out in Bethlehem!

2. The revolving door was invented by a Philadelphia native named Theophilus Van Kannel. Kannel patented the first revolving door in 1888. He allegedly invented it because it cut down on drafts, though it has been rumored that his real reason for inventing it was he hated holding doors for women. He won several awards for his invention, including an award from the Franklin Institute in Philadelphia.

3. Benjamin invented the lightning rod back in 1749, later making advancements to his technology in 1760. His invention came about thanks to his research on electricity and his desire to stop fires from happening in Philadelphia.

4. Modern streetlights were another one of Benjamin Franklin's inventions. During his time, there were streetlights but they were globes, which got dirty really fast and didn't give off a whole lot of light. Franklin came up with the idea of four panes of flat glass, which paved the way to the modern streetlights we all know of today.

5. We can also credit Ben Franklin with designing bifocal glasses. He came up with the invention back in 1748 so that he wouldn't have to change back and forth between up-close and distance glasses. Combining the two has made life easier for people from all around the world — and we have the (most genius) Philadelphian inventor to thank!

6. The polio vaccine was invented by Dr. Jonas Salk, who was working as a medical researcher at the University of Pittsburgh School of Medicine. It took seven years for Dr. Salk and his team to design the vaccine, which he first tested on himself and his family. Salk's invention reduced the number of polio cases from approximately 29,000 in 1955 to less than 6,000 in 1957.

7. The first smiley face emoticon was invented by a Carnegie Mellon University research professor named Scott Fahlman in the 1980s. Fahlman invented the sideways smiley face, which he added for fun to emails, chats, and newsgroup posts. This paved the way for the emojis and animated emojis that we've all come to take for granted today.

8. Although the first lighter wasn't invented in the state, Pennsylvania native George Blaisdell founded the Zippo Manufacturing Company back in 1932. The Zippo lighter is the most popular lighter in the United States.

9. While he was living in Philadelphia, Benjamin Franklin invented the modern odometer. Franklin designed it to help him determine distance while he was setting up the postal service, which was another one of his inventions.

10. Book matches were invented in Pennsylvania back in 1889. The credit goes to Charles Bowman of Lebanon, Pennsylvania.

11. The Choco Taco was invented in Pennsylvania. The popular ice cream truck treat was created by a Philadelphian named Alan Drazen. Drazen was a Good Humor ice cream truck driver before he later worked in management at the Jack & Jill Company. Rumor has it that he came up with the

invention when envisioning an ice cream taco while he was on vacation.

12. The ice cream soda was invented in Pennsylvania. The credit goes to Robert M. Green, who was running a soda fountain at the Franklin Institute in Philadelphia. Green was making drinks out of syrup, cream, and carbonated water. At one point, Green ran out of cream so he bought ice cream from another vendor. He scooped the ice cream into the glasses of pop and the line at his stand grew rapidly. The rest is history.

13. The first commercial radio broadcast was aired on a Pennsylvania radio station. It happened back in November of 1920 on KDKA in Pittsburgh. The station, which is still around today, aired the results of the presidential election between Warren G. Harding and James M. Cox. It gave information on where people could read about the election in the paper the following day. KDKA continued to broadcast regularly.

14. Perforated toilet paper on individual rolls was invented by Irvin and Clarence Scott of Scott's Paper Company in Philadelphia in 1890.

15. The Jeep was invented in Pennsylvania. At the beginning of World War II, the United States army

wanted someone to invent an all-purpose, all-terrain, 4wD vehicle. The American Bantam Car Company, which was located in Butler, PA, was the company to fulfill this requirement. It was tested by then-Colonel Dwight D. Eisenhower in 1941 and was mass produced shortly after.

16. The Heinz company, which is based in Pittsburgh, was the first company to ever produce tomato-based ketchup. Pre-packaged ketchup made its debut back in 1859.

17. The No. 2 pencil was invented by a Philadelphian in 1858. Hymen Lipman came up with the idea of combining the pencil and the eraser.

18. The Crayola company, which is located in Easton, PA, didn't invent crayons. In 1903, Crayola became the first to sell crayons, however.

19. A Philadelphian by the name of William Wrigley, Jr. founded Juicy Fruit gum back in 1891.

20. *TV Guide* magazine got started in Philadelphia. The guide, which was created in 1953, came out during a time when most people didn't even own TVs.

Test Yourself – Questions

1. Which of the following foods was _not_ brought to Pennsylvania by German settlers?

   a. Scrapple
   b. Philly Cheesesteaks
   c. Pretzels

2. The Banana Split was invented by:

   a. A restaurant owner
   b. A dairy farmer
   c. A pharmacist's apprentice

3. Dr. Jonas Salk, who worked at the University of Pittsburgh School of Medicine, invented the vaccine for which of the following diseases?

   a. Measles
   b. HPV
   c. Polio

4. Which famous fast food chain item was invented in Pennsylvania?

   a. The Big Mac
   b. The Whopper
   c. The Chalupa

5. While the first Ferris Wheel was designed by a Pennsylvanian, it was created for a fair in which of the following cities?

   a. Houston, Texas
   b. Chicago, Illinois
   c. Boston, Massachusetts

Answers

1. b.

2. c.

3. c.

4. a.

5. b.

CHAPTER FOUR

PENNSYLVANIA'S ATTRACTIONS

Whether you're planning a trip to Pennsylvania, you might be wondering what attractions the Keystone State has to offer. Do you know which museum is home to a unique cultural artifact? Do you know which historical home is a top Philadelphia tourist attraction? Do you know about the unique theme park based on a children's TV series in the state? Read on to find out the answers to these and other questions.

Hersheypark Holds This Leading Record

Did you know that Hersheypark holds the record for the highest number of visitors each year out of any privately-owned amusement park in the United States? In 2017, the park saw 3.3 million visitors.

The theme park, which was originally a leisure and picnic area for Milton S. Hershey's employees, opened its first roller coaster in 1923. It was a wooden roller coaster that was called the Wild Cat.

In 1977, Hersheypark opened the Sooperdooperlooper, which was the first looping roller coaster on the East Coast.

Since then, the park has gone on to accumulate more than 70 rides and attractions. The park is also home to ZooAmerica, which is home to a number of types of animals.

One of the park's biggest draws is Hershey's Chocolate World, which is located adjacent to the park. There, you'll find marketplace shops and restaurants, which specialize in Hershey's chocolate products. It also offers a chocolate factory-themed tour ride.

A Crayon Museum in Pennsylvania is Home to the World's Largest Crayon

The Crayola Experience is a popular tourist attraction, especially for families with young children. The Crayola Experienced is located in Easton, PA at a location separate from the Crayola company's main manufacturing plant in Forks Township, PA.

The Crayola Experience is a museum and visitor center that helps people learn more about Crayola's history and products. It's also home to a "discovery center," which helps you learn more about the manufacturing process of crayons.

In 2013, the Crayola Experience revealed one of its most unique attractions: "The World's Largest Crayon." The crayon, which is 15 feet long and weighs 1,500 pounds, was made from leftover crayon bits from children across American. The crayon is blue. Today, you can take a photo with the oversized crayon.

You Can See Where the Declaration of Independence and the U.S. Constitution Were Signed in PA

If you're a history buff, then a trip to Pennsylvania isn't complete without a visit to Independence Hall.

When you visit Independence Hall, which was previously known as the Pennsylvania State Room, you can visit the Assembly Room. It was here that the Declaration of Independence and the U.S. Constitution were both signed. It might surprise you to learn that Abraham Lincoln's body was kept in this room for two days after he was assassinated.

At Independence Hall, you'll also find the Courtroom of the Pennsylvania Supreme Court, which was used during the 1700s. This room also once served as the National Museum, where artifacts were kept in honor of the nation's independence.

Independence Hall's Long Gallery once served as a reception area for those who wanted to meet with the state's governor. It also served as a hospital for wounded American prisoners of war and later Peale's Museum, which was one of the first museums in the country.

The Governor's Council Chamber is home to a surveyor's tool that was once used by Charles Manson and Jeremiah Dixon.

The Committee of the Assembly Chamber was a place where slave fugitives were held for trial.

You Won't Hear the Liberty Bell Ring When You're in Philadelphia

The Liberty Bell Center is one of Philadelphia's top attractions. More than a million people from throughout the world visit the bell each year.

There's no doubt that the Liberty Bell is a symbol of America's independence. The bell, which was once located in the steeple of Independence Hall, can now be found in the Liberty Bell Center in Independence National Historical Park.

A common misconception is that the Liberty Bell was rung on July 4th, 1776. This couldn't have happened because the Second Continental Congress's vote for independence wasn't announced until later. Bells were rung on July 8th to celebrate the reading of the Declaration of Independence and while most historians believe that the Liberty Bell was indeed rung that day, there's not actually any proof or documentation that confirms this ever happened.

You might also be disappointed to learn that you probably won't get to hear the Liberty Bell ring during your next trip to Philadelphia. In fact, the bell hasn't been rung since 1846 in honor of George Washington's celebration. The bell's "fatal" crack also happened in 1846.

Longwood Gardens Was Founded by the du Pont Family

The du Pont family has been one of the richest families in all of America since the 19th century. Known for founding one of the largest chemical companies, it's a little-known fact to many that the du Pont family also founded Longwood Gardens, Philadelphia's most popular botanical garden.

It all started out in 1906 when Pierre S. du Pont originally purchased the farm that is today Longwood Gardens to preserve the trees, which were about to be cut down by a lumber mill. Du Pont wanted the space to entertain his friends. He didn't know at the time that Longwood Gardens would one day be one of the top botanical gardens in the country.

Spanning across more than 1,000 acres, Longwood Gardens was one of the first botanical gardens in the United States.

The beautifully landscaped gardens feature an indoor children's garden, Italian water garden, waterfalls, fountains, a waterlily pond, a museum, a greenhouse, and other gorgeous displays that change according to the season.

Longwood Gardens is home to a number of seasonal themes: the Orchid Extravaganza, Spring Blooms, Festival of Fountains, Autumn's Colors, A Longwood Christmas, and Garden Railway.

America's First Zoo Can Be Found in Pennsylvania

Did you know that the first "true" zoo to ever open in the United States can be found in the Keystone State?

The Philadelphia Zoo was opened in July of 1874. Its opening was delayed by the American Civil War.

When the zoo first opened, it was the first of its kind. It started out as a home to 1,000 animals and charged an admission fee of 25 cents.

The zoo's animal population hasn't grown much. Today, the zoo is home to almost 1,300 animals.

The Philadelphia Zoo is most well-known for its breeding program. The zoo is known to breed animals that are considered difficult to breed in captivity. It has been home to the following animal birth records:

- The first successful orangutan-chimpanzee hybrid (1928).
- The first cheetahs to ever be born at a zoo (1956).
- The first successful birth of an echidna in North America (1983).
- The first giant river otter birth in North America (2004).

The Philadelphia Zoo is also known for being home to the first captive flamingos. It was also the first zoo to ever successfully breed Chilean flamingos and greater flamingos in captivity.

In 1983, the zoo also began the Guam Bird Rescue Project. The project was an effort designed to save the Guam Kingfisher and the Guam rail, two bird species native to Guam that were facing extinction due to the introduction of the brown tree snake on the island.

The Philadelphia Zoo has been consistently ranked as one of the top zoos in America, along with the San Diego Zoo.

Pennsylvania is Home to One of the Strangest Museums in the World

There are some pretty strange museums out there in the world—and Pennsylvania is home to one of them!

The Mütter Museum in Philadelphia has a number of... well, *weird*... exhibitions. The museum has more than 20,000 human skulls, human skeletons, body parts, tumors and cysts in just about every organ in the body, and other unusual medical artifacts on display.

Some of the most bizarre pieces on display at the museum include:

- Slides of Albert Einstein's brain.
- Tissue from John Wilkes Booth, Abraham Lincoln's assassin.
- A man's skull badly eaten away by tertiary syphilis.
- The Mütter American Giant, a 7'6" human skeleton.
- President Grover Cleveland's malignant tumor of the hard palate.
- The posterior torso and conjoined liver that belonged to Siamese twins Chang and Eng Bunker.

Dr. Thomas Dent Mütter donated the museum's original collection back in 1858. It was intended to be for medical research and education.

The Philadelphia Museum of Art is Home to This Unique Attraction

The Philadelphia Museum of Art is one of the city's most popular tourist attractions, drawing in more than 800,000 people each year.

The museum has more than 240,000 objects, including American, European, and Asian artworks. In terms of gallery space, the Philadelphia Museum of Art is one of the largest museums in the entire world. It also houses the most important collection of Auguste Rodin's works, outside of Paris, France can be found at the museum.

But there's one attraction that sets the Philadelphia Museum of Art apart from others. The South Asian Art Gallery is the only place in the world that you can see an Indian temple outside of India.

The Pillared Temple Hall dates back to 1560. It came from the Madana Gopala Swamy Temple in Madurai, India. It's believed that the temple was built by a ruler from the Nayaka Dynasty, who had control over Madurai between the mid-1500s and mid-1700s.

It's thought that the 64 granite pieces in the hall were either dismantled or fell and were piled up as rubble, as there is damage that's visible on them today.

You're probably wondering how the temple got to the Philadelphia Museum of Art. Well, in 1912, Adeline Pepper Gibson, who was the daughter of a wealthy Philadelphian family, went to Madurai for her honeymoon. While she was there, she purchased 64 carved granite pieces of the temple. While it's illegal to export ancient artworks from India today without permission from the government, that law didn't exist back in 1912 when Gibson made her purchase.

The pieces were shipped to Philadelphia four years later, during World War I. Adeline Pepper Gibson, whose marriage had been annulled, had traveled to France to establish an army hospital. While she was there in 1919, she died of pneumonia. Her family was unsure of what to do with her purchase from Madurai and decided to donate it to the Philadelphia Museum of Art in her honor.

Camelback Mountain is Known for Its Water Parks

Pennsylvania is home to a number of water parks, but Camelbeach in Tannersville, PA is the largest in the state!

Camelbeach Mountain Water Park is operated during the summer by Camelback Mountain, the largest ski resort in the Poconos. Camelbeach Mountain Water Park is home to 37 water slides, rides, and other attractions.

Camelbeach offers a number of water rides, including tube slides, raft slides, bowl water slides, a mat slide, a lazy river, and a wave pool.

TripSavvy ranks Camelbeach Mountain Water Park as one of the two best water parks in the state (the other being The Boardwalk at Hersheypark).

Camelback also offers an indoor water park, which is called Aquatopia. In 2015, *USA Today* ranked Aquatopia the #1 indoor water park in the country.

The Oldest Book Shop in America is Located in Pennsylvania

Did you know that the oldest bookshop in America and the 2nd oldest bookshop in the entire *world* can be found in the Keystone State?

The Moravian Book Shop, which is located in Bethlehem, holds the record for the oldest continuously operating bookstore in the country and the 2nd oldest in the world. (The first oldest is the Livraria Bertrand in Lisbon, Portugal, which was founded in 1732).

Founded in 1745 by the Moravian Church, the church owned the bookshop for 273 years! When it first started out, the bookstore provided devotional and liturgical materials to the church for missionaries, churchgoers, and students. Since it was founded, the book shop's location has changed several times, including its temporary home in Philadelphia at one point, where it also printed books.

The Moravian Book Shop moved to its current location on Main Street in historic Downtown Bethlehem back in 1871. The store has expanded over time, now taking up four buildings and 14,000 square feet.

In 2018, the Moravian Church Northern Province decided to sell the bookshop to Moravian College—a decision that was made to keep the bookshop in the "Moravian Family" so that the church could focus on its 85 congregations.

Today, the Moravian Book Shop is home to the Moravian College student bookstore. It sells both books and apparel to Moravian College students. The bookstore also sells trade books, Indie best-sellers, and books focused on the history of Bethlehem, the Lehigh Valley, Pennsylvania, and more.

Pittsburgh Zoo & PPG Aquarium is One of Only Six Zoo and Aquarium Combinations in America

Did you know that the Pittsburgh Zoo & PPG Aquarium is one of only *six* zoo and aquarium combinations in the USA?

The zoo is home to more than 4,000 animals, including 20 species which are endangered or threatened.

The Pittsburgh Zoo opened back in 1898 when politician Christopher Lyman Magee donated $125,000 for a zoological garden to be built in Highland Park. The zoo was originally named the Highland Park Zoo.

Since the zoo opened, it's become home to a number

of exhibits. It has also gained attention for its tiger breeding program.

PPG Aquarium was added to the zoo in 1967. The two-story aquarium is home to a number of exhibits, such as a tropical rainforest and fish and aquatic species specific to Pennsylvania's Allegheny River.

Gettysburg National Military Park Preserves One of the Nation's Most Important Battlefields

If you're a history buff, then you probably already know that the Battle of Gettysburg was one of the most significant battles fought during the American Civil War. Today, you can visit Gettysburg National Military Park to learn more about the historical battle.

The Gettysburg Museum of the Civil War is the park's biggest attraction. The museum has the largest collection of Civil War artifacts, including those from both the Battle of Gettysburg and Civil War veterans. You will also get to see a film called *A New Birth of Freedom*, which is narrated by Morgan Freeman.

You can also take a guided tour of the battlefield, which will help you learn more about the Battle of Gettysburg.

Ricketts Glen State Park Has a Rich History

Ricketts Glen State Park is one of the most popular state parks in Pennsylvania. Located in Sullivan, Luzerne, and Columbia counties in PA, the state park is recognized as a National Natural Landmark. Situated on13,050 acres of land, the park is known for its old-growth forest and its 24 named waterfalls.

Ricketts Glen State Park has a rich history. Did you know that it was once home to Native Americans? The region was once home to the Susquehannock people and, later, the Iroquois. In 1768, the British acquired the area from the Iroquois in the New Purchase.

The Ricketts family were on a hunting trip in the area in 1850 when they were upset about having to sleep on the parlor floor at a hotel. The Ricketts brothers, Elijah and Clemuel, decided to buy 5,000 acres of land in the area as a hunting preserve, including some of what is the park today and Lake Ganoga.

Elijah's son, Robert Bruce Ricketts, went on to purchase the land from him in 1869. Robert soon owned or had control over more than 60,000 acres in the area. He opened the North Mountain House hotel in 1873, which remained open until1903. The waterfalls in the area were one of the hotel's biggest attractions. Robert Bruce Ricketts built the trail along the waterfalls.

Ricketts opened the waterfalls and glen to the public in 1913, charging $1 for admission.

Robert Bruce Ricketts died in 1918.

During the 1930s, there were plans to make Ricketts Glen a national park. The funding was unavailable after World War II, however.

The Pennsylvania Game Commission began to purchase the land from Ricketts' heirs in 1942. When the state park was established in 1944, it was named after Ricketts.

You Can Visit the Birthplace of the American Flag in PA

Did you know that you can visit the birthplace of the American flag during your next trip to Pennsylvania?

Located in Philadelphia's Historic District, the Betsy Ross House is where the country's most famous seamstress and flag maker is said to have lived when she sewed the first American flag. Known as the Betsy Ross flag, Ross's early design of the American flag featured 13 stars (to represent each of the 13 original colonies) in a circle design.

Although some historians disagree that Ross actually lived in the house when she sewed the first flag, her ancestors are the ones who claimed this was her residence at the time. It's believed that Betsy Ross resided in the home from 1776 to 1779.

Today, the Betsy Ross House is one of the most visited tourist sites in Philadelphia.

The "Niagara Falls of Pennsylvania" is Located in the Poconos

If you're a nature lover, then you may be wondering where the most beautiful waterfalls in all of Pennsylvania can be found. Well, look no further. Bushkill Falls, which is located in the Poconos, is often referred to as the "Niagara Falls of Pennsylvania."

The eight privately owned waterfalls opened to the public in 1904 by Charles E. Peters. The falls still remain in the Peters family to this day.

The falls are named Bushkill Falls, Bridal Veil Falls, bridesmaid Falls, Laurel Glen Falls, and Pennell Falls. Three of the falls don't have names.

Bushkill Falls is a popular spot for hiking in the area, with a variety of trails and bridges. It's often said that a trip to the Poconos is incomplete without a trip to see the falls!

RANDOM FACTS

1. The Big Mac Museum is located in North Huntingdon, Pennsylvania. Located near where the classic fast food item was originally developed, the museum opened back in 2007 inside a McDonald's restaurant (which is fully functioning). While you grab some lunch, you can check out some artifacts related to the sandwich's history and creation.

2. The longest-operating drive-in movie theater in the entire United States of America can be found in Orefield, Pennsylvania. Shankweiler's Drive-In opened back in 1934.

3. Sesame Place, which is located in Langhorne, PA, is the only theme park in the world that's based on the TV show *Sesame Street*. The children's theme park has rides, water rides, and shows. It's owned and operated by SeaWorld Entertainment.

4. The Andy Warhol Museum is the largest museum in the entire U.S. that's devoted to a single artist. Located in Pittsburgh, the museum is dedicated to pop art icon Andy Warhol—who was a Pittsburgh native!

5. Benjamin Franklin Parkway is a scenic boulevard that runs through Philadelphia. Named after Benjamin Franklin, the mile-long parkway starts at Philadelphia City Hall, runs through Logan Circle, and ends right before the Philadelphia Museum of Art.

6. Famous architect Frank Lloyd Wright's Fallingwater, which is considered to be his biggest masterpiece of all-time, is located in Stewart Township, PA. The *Smithsonian* listed the house, which rests above a waterfall, as one of its "28 Places to See Before You Die."

7. Penn's Landing in Philadelphia is a waterfront area along the Delaware River. The Great Plaza at Penn's Landing is a popular spot for outdoor concerts and festivals.

8. There are a number of great ways to ring in the New Year in Pennsylvania. You might not find a ball being dropped in the state, but instead, you'll find a giant Hershey's Kiss in Hershey, a giant Peep in Bethlehem, a wrench in Mechanicsburg, 200 pounds of bologna in Lebanon, glowing coal in Shamokin, and a huge pair of yellow pants in Lower Allen Township.

9. The Franklin Institute is a science museum in Philadelphia. It's also a science education and research center. Named after Benjamin Franklin,

the Franklin Institute is one of America's oldest science education centers. It opened in 1954. The museum is most well-known for its exhibit *The Giant Heart.*

10. Quiet Valley Farm is a historic working farm, which operates a museum. Located in Hamilton Township near Stroudsburg in the Poconos, the farm teaches people about life from the 1760s to 1913.

11. The Barnes Foundation, which is located in Philadelphia, is an educational institution and art collection that is home to more than 4,000 pieces.

12. Knoebels Amusement Resort is a family-owned amusement park, which also offers a campground and picnic area. Located in Elysburg, PA, Knoebels is the largest free-admission amusement park in the United States. Some of the park's rides include a steel roller coaster, three wooden roller coasters, and a carousel that was built in 1913.

13. Phipps Conservatory and Botanical Gardens was given to the city of Pittsburgh as a gift by its founder, steel and real-estate magnate, Henry Phipps.

14. Dorney Park & Wildwater Kingdom is an amusement park and water park that's located in Allentown, Pennsylvania. The park is well-known for its roller coasters. Dorney's most

famous roller coaster is Steel Force, which is the 2nd longest steel roller coaster on the U.S. East Coast and the 9th longest in the entire world.

15. Kennywood Park, which is located in West Mifflin, was originally opened as a trolley park attraction. Today, it's one of only 13 trolley parks that are still operating in the country.

16. Glen Onoko Falls in Jim Thorpe is considered to be one of the state's most scenic hiking spots.

17. Mount Airy Casino Resort in Mount Pocono, PA and Sands Casino Resort in Bethlehem are the most popular casino resorts in the state.

18. Bartram's Garden, which was started by botanist John Bartram back in 1728, is the oldest surviving botanical garden in America.

19. Elfreth's Alley in Philadelphia is the oldest road in America that has been continuously inhabited. The street was built in 1702, with its 32 houses being built between 1728 and 1836.

20. New Hope in Bucks County, PA is known for its famous New Hope & Ivyland Railroad train rides.

Test Yourself – Questions

1. Which of the following was the first zoo in America?

    a. The Pittsburgh Zoo
    b. The Philadelphia Zoo
    c. The Highland Park Zoo

2. The oldest bookshop in the country (and the second oldest in the world) is located in which of the following towns?

    a. Philadelphia, PA
    b. Allentown, PA
    c. Bethlehem, PA

3. Which of Pennsylvania's attractions was listed as one of the *Smithsonian*'s "28 Places to See Before You Die"?

    a. Fallingwater
    b. Bushkill Falls
    c. Glen Ricketts State Park

4. The longest-operating drive-in in the United States is located in which of Pennsylvania's towns?

    a. Scranton, PA
    b. Orefield, PA
    c. Mount Pocono, PA

5. Slides of Albert Einstein's brain can be found at which museum in Philadelphia, PA?

   a. The Philadelphia Museum of Art
   b. The Franklin Institute
   c. The Mütter Museum

Answers

1. b.
2. c.
3. a.
4. b.
5. c.

CHAPTER FIVE

PENNSYLVANIA'S SPORTS

It has been said that Pennsylvania sports fans are some of the most passionate sports fans in the entire United States. If you ever decide to attend a game in the state, you might find this to be true! How much do you know about sports in Pennsylvania? Do you know which sports legends are from the Keystone State? To find out the answers to these and other questions, read on!

The First Baseball Stadium Was Built in Pennsylvania

Baseball may have been invented in Cooperstown, New York, but did you know that the first baseball stadium was actually built in Pennsylvania?

The stadium was built in Forbes Field in the Oakland neighborhood of Pittsburgh back in 1909.

Forbes Field served as the third home to the MLB team the Pittsburgh Pirates, as well as the first home of the NFL team the Pittsburgh Steelers. The University of Pittsburgh Panthers also used it as their home football field.

Barney Dreyfuss, who was the owner of the Pittsburgh Pirates, was the imitator of the project. The stadium was named after John Forbes, a British general who named the city of Pittsburgh in 1758.

The stadium was the first ballpark to ever be made entirely of steel and concrete, a move that was made to increase its lifespan. The stadium had a number of luxury features that were some of the first of its kind, including elevators and luxury suites.

In June of 1970, the Pittsburgh Pirates and the Chicago Cubs played the final game in Forbes Field. That being said, some of the ballpark still remains. Today, it's surrounded by the campus of the University of Pittsburgh.

A Pennsylvania Team Played in the First World Series

Did you know that a Pennsylvania team played in the first World Series of Major League Baseball?

In 1903, the Pittsburgh Pirates played against the Boston Americans.

The first World Series was played in Pennsylvania, too. The game was held at Exposition Park in Pittsburgh.

The game, which was played best-of-nine, was won by the Boston Americans. The Americans beat the Pirates five to three.

Professional Football Kind of Started Out in Pennsylvania

It might surprise you to learn that some of the biggest historical records in professional football history trace back to Pennsylvania.

William "Pudge" Heffelfinger was the first known professional football player in history, and he played for the Allegheny Athletic Association in 1892.

John Brallier was the first openly paid professional football player. Brallier earned $10 to play for the Latrobe Athletic Association back in 1895.

In 1896, the Allegheny Athletic Association became home to the first openly paid professional team.

Then in 1902, three Pennsylvania teams formed the National Football League. Not to be confused with the National Football League of today, this early league was the first attempt at establishing a national professional football league.

One Pennsylvania Town is Named After an Athlete

Did you know that one town in the Keystone State was named after an athlete who came from the state?

Jim Thorpe was the first Native American to win an Olympic gold medal. In 1912, Thorpe won Olympic gold medals in the pentathlon and decathlon.

Thorpe, who has been called one of the most versatile athletes of all time, also played football and baseball. A Major League Baseball player, he played for both the New York Giants who later sold him to the Cincinnati Reds. Thorpe returned to the Giants before later being sold to the (then) Boston Braves.

As a football player, Thorpe played for six NFL teams over the course of his career. He later went on to coach several NFL football teams.

Jim Thorpe was the first president of the American Professional Association (today's National Football League), a position which he began in 1920 and ended in 1921.

Thorpe also played professional basketball.

Jim Thorpe was a professional athlete until he was 41 years old. His athletic career ended when the Great Depression began.

Jim Thorpe was inducted into the Pro Football Hall of Fame in 1963.

In addition to starring in several movies himself, there was a film about his life, titled *Jim Thorpe – All-American*. Burt Lancaster portrayed Thorpe in the movie.

The town of Jim Thorpe in Pennsylvania is named in the late athlete's honor. There's a monument site in the town at the site of where his remains lie.

While Jim Thorpe was from Oklahoma, he attended the Carlisle Indian Industrial School in Carlisle, PA. The school was the leading boarding school for Native Americans until 1918.

There's a Huge Rivalry Between Fans of These PA NFL Teams

Many states have a rivalry between fans of two major sports teams, whether it be at the college or professional level. In Pennsylvania, there's a huge rivalry between fans of the Pittsburgh Steelers and the Philadelphia Eagles.

The Pittsburgh Steelers are one of the most popular NFL teams in the entire United States. Their fans are considered to be the most loyal of all NFL fans and are known as "The Steelers Nation." Although the Steelers have fans throughout the whole country, their fans in Pennsylvania and in the Pittsburgh area tend to even more dedicated.

The Philadelphia Eagles don't have as much nationwide fandom as the Steelers do. In Pennsylvania and especially within the Philadelphia area, however, the Philadelphia Eagles have a very strong and loyal fan base. Eagles fans are known to be passionate and dedicated about their team. They're also known to get pretty rowdy at times. In fact, Veterans Stadium, which was once home field to the Eagles, was the first U.S. sports stadium to ever have a jail cell for its rowdy fans. The jail cell was eventually removed.

Both Steelers and Eagles fans are known to go the distance for their team. When the teams play far away from home, both Steelers and Eagles fans tend to travel. In fact, it's been said that opposing teams often feel as though they're not in their own home stadium because both teams produce a large number of passionate fans at away games.

But the Eagles and Steelers Actually Once Played Together as a Single Team

Most Eagles and Steelers fans would cringe at the idea of their two teams playing together, but it actually happened at one point in history!

The Philadelphia Eagles and Pittsburgh Steelers once merged together to form the "Steagles." This decision was made during World War II in an attempt at keeping the NFL alive when so many men had been sent off to fight in the war. The managers of both teams decided to this as a way of making sure that there was at least one NFL team in Pennsylvania.

We know what you're thinking. If this happened

today, it would *not* be a popular move. Well, it wasn't then, either.

Pennsylvania's NFL Teams Have Won the Super Bowl Seven Times

Did you know that Pennsylvania's NFL teams have won the Super Bowl a total of seven times?

Six of those Super Bowls were won by the Pittsburgh Steelers. As of 2018, the Steelers have the highest number of Super Bowl wins in the NFL!

The Pittsburgh Steelers have played in the Super Bowl a total of 8 times, losing only two of them. Four of the Super Bowl games that the Steelers won were over the course of six years.

Here's a list of the Steelers' wins:

1. 1975 – The Pittsburgh Steelers beat the Minnesota Vikings, 16-6.
2. 1976 – The Pittsburgh Steelers beat the Dallas Cowboys, 21-17.
3. 1979 – The Pittsburgh Steelers beat the Dallas Cowboys, 35-31.
4. 1980 – The Pittsburgh Steelers beat the Los Angeles Rams, 31-19.
5. 2006 – The Pittsburgh Steelers beat the Seattle Seahawks, 21-10.
6. 2009 – The Pittsburgh Steelers beat the Arizona Cardinals, 27-23.

It was a long-held belief that the Philadelphia Eagles would never win a Super Bowl game, but they proved the world wrong in 2018 when they beat the New England Patriots with a score of 41-33.

This Legendary Professional Golfer Was From PA

Arnold Palmer is recognized as one of the greatest professional golfers of all time. Palmer earned the nickname "The King" and for good reason. He was the first superstar of golf's TV age, which dates back to the 1950s. In addition, he is still regarded as one of the most popular golfers of all-time and is often seen as a trailblazer of the sport. But did you know that Palmer was from the Keystone State?

Born in Latrobe Pennsylvania, Palmer learned to golf at the Latrobe Country Club where his father was head professional and greenskeeper. His father Deacon Palmer taught him how to play while he maintained the golf course.

Arnold Palmer later went on to attend Wake Forest College. His tuition was paid for on a golf scholarship. His time at the college was cut short when he lost his friend Bud and decided to enlist in the U.S. Coast Guard instead.

While he was at the Coast Guard Training Center in Cape May, New Jersey, Palmer built a nine-hole golf course and continued with the sport. Once his coast guard enlistment was over, Palmer went back to college and began to play competitive golf.

In 1945, Arnold Palmer decided to quit his job selling paint and turn pro. He made the decision after winning the 1954 Amateur in Detroit, which gave him the confidence to compete. He played in the Waite Memorial tournament in Shawnee-on-Delaware, Pennsylvania. It was there that he met his future wife of 45 years, Winifred Walzer.

The rest is history. Over the course of his 60-year pro golfing career, Palmer won 62 PGA Tour Titles. He also won seven major titles: four masters, two British Opens, and one U.S. Open. Palmer won the PGA Tour Lifetime Achievement Award in 1998 and he was also one of the first 13 professional golfers to be inducted into the World Golf Hall of Fame.

Arnold Palmer had a significant impact on the popularization and commercialization of professional golf as a sport. He was one of "The Big Three" (along with Gary Player and Jack Nicklaus) who helped popularize the sport during the 1960s.

And to think that it all started in Latrobe, PA!

This NBA Legend is From Pennsylvania

Today, he's widely regarded as one of the best NBA players in history. Over the course of his 20-year long basketball career, during which he played exclusively for the Los Angeles Lakers, he won five NBA championships. But did you know that Kobe Bryant is from Pennsylvania?

Kobe Bryant was born in Philadelphia. His father, Joe Bryant, is also a former NBA player, who played for the Los Angeles Lakers as well.

Kobe Bryant started playing basketball when he was just a toddler. When he was growing up, Bryant was a Lakers fan. His grandfather would mail him videos of NBA games, which Kobe studied.

When Kobe was six years old, Joe Bryant retired from the NBA and moved the family to Rieti, Italy where he continued to play professional basketball. Kobe quickly adapted to this new lifestyle and started speaking fluent Italian. During the summers, Kobe came back to the United States to play basketball in a summer league.

The family moved back to the United States when Joe Bryant retired from basketball in Italy in 1991.

Kobe Bryant went to Lower Merion High School in Ardmore, PA, a Philadelphia suburb. There, he played basketball and gained recognition as the top basketball player of any U.S. high school.

Bryant entered the NBA immediately following high school. Though he was originally drafted by the Charlotte Hornets, they traded him to the Lakers.

By his second season, Bryant was named an All-Star. Bryant and fellow player Shaquille O'Neal led the Lakers to three consecutive NBA championships between 2000 and 2002.

When he was 34 years old, Kobe Bryant became the youngest NBA player in history to ever reach 30,000 career points. In 2010, he also became the all-time leading scoring in Lakers history. He started the All-Star game 18 consecutive times over the course of his career.

Kobe Bryant also won gold medals as a part of the U.S. national team during the 2008 and 2012 Summer Olympics.

In 2018, Kobe Bryant wrote and narrated an animated film called *Dear Basketball*, which is based on his retirement in 2015. The film earned him an Academy Award for Best Animated Short Film.

Despite sexual assault allegations brought against Kobe Bryant in 2003, many sports fans still consider him one of the greatest basketball players of all time—and it all started out in the Keystone State!

This NFL Player from PA Was Almost a Basketball Player Instead

Whether you love sports or hate them, there's a good chance you've probably heard of Joe "The Comeback Kid" Montana. Joe Montana is a former NFL player who played for both the San Francisco 49ers and the Kansas City Chiefs. But did you know that the Pennsylvania native's career almost took a completely different direction?

Montana was born in New Eagle, located in Western PA. He grew up in Monongahela, PA, a coal mining town south of Pittsburgh. Montana attended Waverly Elementary, Finleyville Junior High (today's Finleyville Middle School), and Ringgold High School in Washington County. While he was growing up, Montana's favorite sport was basketball. His father even formed a basketball team, which he played on.

While Joe was in high school, Montana played football, baseball, and basketball. He had success during his high school basketball career, earning the name of an all-state player and helping the team win boys' basketball championship in 1973.

He was offered a basketball scholarship from North Carolina State. Even though Joe Montana ended up turning the scholarship down, he gave it a lot of thought because he would have been able to play both basketball and football for the university.

While he was in high school, Montana didn't see immediate success in football. When he was a freshman and a sophomore, he was a backup player for the Ringgold High School football team. It wasn't until he was a junior that he finally got to play as the team's starting quarterback. He remained starting quarterback throughout his junior and senior years. *Parade* named Joe Montana to their All-American team after his senior year.

During his junior year, Montana completed 12 passes, threw for 223 yards, and scored 3 passing touchdowns and a rushing touchdown. His performance in the game earned him interest from college recruiters, including Notre Dame, who Montana accepted a scholarship from.

During the course of his NFL career, Joe Montana achieved a number of accomplishments. He was the first player in NFL history to be named the Super Bowl Most Valuable Player three times. He still holds the Super Bowl record for most passes without an interception. In 2000, he was elected to the Pro Football Hall of Fame. *ESPN* also named Joe Montana the "25th greatest athlete of the 20th century" back in 1999.

Montana's memory is carried alive at Ringgold High School to this day. In 2006, Ringgold High School's football stadium was renamed "Joe Montana Stadium" in the former NFL player's honor.

This Famous Professional Skateboarder is from PA

Today, he's most well-known for starring in all three *Jackass* movies, as well as his reality TV shows, *Viva La Bam* and *Bam's Unholy Union*. But did you know that before he rose to fame, West Chester native Bam Margera originally started out recording videos of himself and his friends riding skateboards and doing skateboarding stunts?

In 1997 and 1998, Bam Margera was a professional skateboarder. He was sponsored by Toy Machine Skateboards.

After his rise to fame as an actor/reality tv star, his career as a professional skateboarder continued.

From 2001 to 2016, Margera was a member of Team Element, which is a demonstration team for Element Skateboards.

In 2017, Margera retired from skateboarding at the professional level. He did continue to skateboard casually, reigniting his partnership with Element Skateboards.

Bam's impact on the skateboarding world is considered to be a significant one—and it all started with the West Chester High School alumni!

This Former MLB Catcher Was from the Keystone State

Did you know that one of the best offensive catchers in MLB history hails from Pennsylvania?

Former MLB catcher Mike Piazza was born in Norristown, PA and grew up in Phoenixville, PA where he attended high school.

Mike Piazza's father helped him learn how to hit, pitching hundreds of baseballs at him every night. They practiced even if there was snow on the ground, clearing a spot to continue with his instruction if needed.

His father wasn't the only one who helped train him. He also received lessons from a Hall of Famer. When Piazza was 12 years old, he received backyard batting cage instruction from former Boston Red Sox player Ted Williams. Williams gave Piazza a lot of praise and encouraged him not to let anyone change his swing.

Though he grew up a Phillies fan, Piazza never played for them. He was initially drafted to the Los Angeles Dodgers as a favor from Tommy Lasorda to Pizza's father. Piazza later went on to play for the Florida Marlins, New York Mets, San Diego Padres, and Oakland Athletics.

While he was playing for the Mets, Mike Piazza had one of the longest runs batted in (RBI) streaks in the history of the MLB with 15 consecutive games. When he was playing for the Dodgers in 1997, he earned the Most Valuable Player Award. Piazza was later inducted into the Mets Hall of Fame and the Baseball Hall of Fame.

Minor League Baseball is a Big Deal in Pennsylvania

Did you know that Pennsylvania is home to 11 minor league baseball teams? Although three of the state's minor league baseball teams are independent, eight of those teams are affiliated with MLB teams.

Here's a list of minor league teams and their affiliated MLB teams:

1. The Lehigh Valley IronPigs are affiliated with the Philadelphia Phillies.
2. The Scranton/Wilkes Barre Railriders are affiliated with the New York Yankees.
3. The Altoona Curve are affiliated with the Pittsburgh Pirates.
4. The Erie SeaWolves are affiliated with the Detroit Tigers.
5. The Harrisburg Senators are affiliated with the Washington Nationals.
6. The Reading Fightin Phils are affiliated with the Philadelphia Phillies.
7. The State College Spikes are affiliated with the St. Louis Cardinals.

8. The Williamsport Crosscutters are affiliated with the Philadelphia Phillies.
9. The Lancaster Barnstormers (independent).
10. The York Revolution (independent).
11. The Washington Wild Things (independent).

A Pennsylvania Team Played in the First Televised NFL Game Ever

Did you know that one of Pennsylvania's NFL teams played in the first NFL game to *ever* be broadcast on television? Can you guess which team it was? You might be surprised to learn that it was *not* the Pittsburgh Steelers.

The Philadelphia Eagles played in the first-ever televised NFL game. In 1939, the Eagles played against the former Brooklyn Football Dodgers. The Philadelphia Eagles lost the game, 23-14.

The game, which was aired on NBC, was only broadcasted in New York City. An estimated 500 New Yorkers watched the commercial-free game, which lasted 2 hours and 33 minutes.

RANDOM FACTS

1. John F. Kennedy and his brothers almost bought the Philadelphia Eagles for an appealing $6 million. However, the deal didn't work out because they didn't believe it would work out with JFK's responsibilities as President of the United States at the time.

2. Pennsylvania is only home to one National Basketball Association (NBA) team. That team is the Philadelphia 76ers, which originally started out in Syracuse, NY. As of 2018, the 76ers have won the 5th highest number of championship games in the history of the NBA, tying only with the Miami Heat and the Detroit Pistons.

3. There was another NBA team in Philadelphia between the years of 1946 and 1962. The Philadelphia Warriors has since moved to San Francisco and is known as the Golden State Warriors today.

4. The Philadelphia Eagles have the only left-facing logo in the NFL. The logo, which made its debut in 1996, features a bird head. The reason it faces the left is that there's a capital "E" in the feathers. In 1996, the Eagles also made the switch from "Kelly green" jerseys to "midnight green."

5. The Pittsburgh Steelers are the oldest franchise in the AFC. The team was founded by Art Rooney in 1933. The team has remained within the Rooney family to this day.

6. When the Pittsburgh Steelers were first founded, they were known as the Pittsburgh Pirates. The team's name was changed in 1940 in an effort to build a stronger fan base. It was clearly successful.

7. Former professional road racing cyclist Floyd Landis is from Farmersville, PA. Landis was the original winner of the 2006 Tour de France cycling tour, but he found himself in the center of some controversy when it was discovered that he had been using performance-enhancing drugs.

8. Former NFL quarterback Joe Namath was from Beaver Falls, PA. Namath played for the New York Jets for the majority of his professional football career, though he retired from the Los Angeles Rams. Namath was inducted into the Pro Football Hall of Fame.

9. Former NFL player Johnny Unitas was from Pittsburgh, Pennsylvania. Also known as "The Golden Arm" and "Johnny U," Unitas spent most of his career playing for the Baltimore Colts. Often recognized as one of the greatest NFL players in history, Johnny U held the record for the most consecutive games with a touchdown pass until it was broken in 2012.

10. Philadelphia Phillies player Rick Wise played what is still considered to be one of the greatest baseball games in the history of the MLB back in June of 1971. Wise hit two home-runs *and* pitched a no-hitter against the Cincinnati Reds. This earned him the record of the first MLB player to ever pitch a no-hitter and hit two home runs in a single game, a record that he's held to this day.

11. Two Pennsylvania MLB teams played the first game that was ever aired on the radio in August of 1921. The game, which the Philadelphia Phillies played against the Pittsburgh Pirates, was called into the radio station by a Pittsburgh DJ named Harold Arlin. Arlin shared the game over the phone. The Pirates won the game with a score of 8-5.

12. The Philadelphia Phillies also played in the first ever nighttime MLB game. They played against the Cincinnati Reds, who beat them 2-1.

13. Pennsylvania's MLB teams have won a combined seven World Series championships. The Pittsburgh Pirates won the World Series in 1909, 1925, 1960, 1971, and 1979. The Philadelphia Phillies won the World Series in 1980 and 2008.

14. The Philadelphia Eagles got their name after Bert Bell and Lud Wray purchased the then-bankrupt Frankford Yellowjackets in 1933. Bell and Wray

renamed the team the Eagles to honor the symbol of President Franklin D. Roosevelt's National Recovery Act.

15. The Philadelphia Phillies were known as the Quakers when the team was founded back in 1883. As times changed, the team became known as the "Philadelphias." This was eventually shortened to the "Phillies," which they officially became known as in 1890.

16. The Philadelphia Sports Hall of Fame was established in 2002 to honor people from the region who have made athletic achievements. It's located at 2701 Grant Avenue in Philadelphia.

17. Pittsburgh may have been home to the first baseball stadium, but it was home to another first when it comes to sports stadiums: a retractable roof on the city's Civic Arena. The idea came from a local businessman by the name of Edgar J. Kaufmann. The arena was originally intended for the Pittsburgh Civic Light Opera when it was built in 1961, but college basketball and ice hockey events took place there as well. In 1967, NHL team the Pittsburgh Penguins formed and the Civic Arena became their home for more than 40 years.

18. Pro Football Hall of Famer and former Philadelphia Eagles player Chuck Bednarik was

born in Bethlehem, PA. Bednarik is regarded as one of the most devastating tacklers in football history, as well as the last NFL player to play both defense and offense.

19. One of the most dominant players in the history of the NBA was from Pennsylvania. Born in Philadelphia, Wilt Chamberlain played for the Philadelphia 76ers, the (then) Philadelphia Warriors, and the Los Angeles Lakers.

20. The Philadelphia 76ers' team name in honor of the signing of the Declaration of Independence in 1776. The team is commonly referred to as the "Sixers," however, as it's easier to remember.

Test Yourself – Questions

1. Which first stadium was *not* built in PA?

    a. The first baseball stadium
    b. The first hockey stadium
    c. The first retractable stadium

2. Joe Montana almost played what sport instead of football?

    a. Baseball
    b. Soccer
    c. Basketball

3. What NFL team in PA holds the record for the highest number of Super Bowl wins in the NFL (as of 2018)?

    a. The Philadelphia Eagles
    b. The Pittsburgh Steelers

4. The team that J.F. Kennedy and his brothers almost bought was:

    a. The Philadelphia Phillies
    b. The Pittsburgh Steelers
    c. The Philadelphia Eagles

5. Pittsburgh Steelers fans are known as:

    a. Steel Nation
    b. Steel Army
    c. The P-Hive

Answers

1. b.
2. c.
3. b.
4. c.
5. a.

CHAPTER SIX

PENNSYLVANIA'S URBAN LEGENDS, UNSOLVED MYSTERIES, AND OTHER WEIRD FACTS!

Every state has its fair share of strange occurrences, unsolved mysteries, and creepy places. Do you know about some of the urban legends and mysteries that haunt the state of Pennsylvania? Do you know what some of the spookiest places in the state are or where you're most likely to encounter some of the most famous ghosts? Warning: this chapter may give you goosebumps. If you're ready to find out some of the strangest and creepiest facts about Pennsylvania, then this chapter is for you.

This Former Prison is Thought to be One of the Most Haunted Places in the U.S.

This haunted attraction is one of the most visited spots in Pennsylvania on Halloween, but did you know that Eastern State Penitentiary is thought to *really* be haunted? In fact, it's believed to be one of the most haunted places in all of America!

Today, the prison is abandoned. However, between the years of 1829 and 1971, when it shut down, 70,000 people were inmates at the facility. Eastern State Penitentiary's history is full of a number of dark things, including torture, murder, and suicide. It's easy to believe that trouble spirits could be haunting the now abandoned facility.

Eastern State Penitentiary was known to use a number of torture methods on its inmates. The facility had a water bath. The inmates were dunked and then hung out on a wall until their skin began to form ice. There was also a mad chair, which inmates were bound to so tightly that they ended up losing circulation and later needed amputations. Then there was the iron gag, in which an iron collar was strapped to the inmate's mouth and his hands were tied behind his back. The inmate couldn't move or he risked the tongue bleeding and tearing. Perhaps the worst torture method yet was "The Hole," which was a dark cell underground. Inmates who spent time in The Hole had no access to light, exercise, toilets, or other humans. They weren't given much food and it was also hard to breathe.

Gary Johnson, who helps maintain the prison's crumbling locks, reported having a ghostly encounter in the early 1990s. Johnson allegedly opened an old lock in Cellblock 4 when he was gripped so tightly by an invisible force that he couldn't even move. He reported a negative energy coming from the cell and faces appearing on the walls.

Of course, there are plenty of skeptics. Some people pass through the prison without experiencing any odd occurrences. Then again, plenty of visitors *do* report odd experiences within the prison's walls— enough people that it's hard to doubt that they could *all* be making it up.

People have claimed to hear voices echoing and cackling noises coming from Cellblock 12. Cellblock 6 is said to be a host of shadow-like silhouettes darting across the walls. In Cellblock 4, you may see ghostly faces. There have also been reported sightings of the silhouette of a guard in one of the prison's towers.

The employees at Eastern State Penitentiary don't claim that the building is haunted, however. They merely run a haunted attraction and don't like to exploit the darker image or the inmates who spent time there.

That being said, a lot of paranormal researchers visit the prison every year. The prison has been featured on a number of TV shows, including *Ghost Adventures* and *Most Haunted Live* on the Travel Channel, *Fear* on MTV, and *Ghost Hunters* on Syfy.

Stroudsburg's Rain Man

One of the creepiest, most baffling unsolved mysteries of all-time happened back in 1983 in a small Pennsylvania town called Stroudsburg. A young man named Don Decker, who was in the middle of serving a 4 to 12-month prison sentence, was released to attend his grandfather's funeral. Decker didn't feel sadness about the death, however, as his grandfather had abused him since he was seven.

Decker was staying with family friends, Bob and Jeannie Keiffer, when things started to get... strange. When Don was in the bathroom the night of the funeral, he got the chills and fainted. He later claimed that he went into a trance-like state and saw his grandfather's spirit above him. Decker also claimed that scratches appeared on his wrists and arms.

Don went downstairs to inform Bob Keiffer about what had happened to him—and that's when things got stranger. There were loud banging noises from upstairs and at that moment, water began to drip down the walls and from the ceiling. The dripping increased until it was raining in the living room. The Keiffers, who were terrified, noticed that Don had gone back into a trance-like state.

Bob Keiffer called his landlord. When the landlord came over, the water just got *worse*. Water began to bubble up through the floor. There were no pipes in the front end of the house that could have caused the leaking. The water flow was strange in that it didn't come from one direction but instead came from all over.

The landlord called the police and officers Richard Wolbert and John Baujan arrived at the scene. They found the mysterious rain falling from the walls and ceiling and noticed something else, too: the water was defying the laws of physics, with some water droplets hovering midair or floating upwards from the floor.

Don Decker had remained in a trance and looked pale and sickly, so the Keiffers took Don to a pizzeria across the street.

As soon as Decker had left the house, the rain stopped.

Things got even stranger when it began to rain at the pizza restaurant, the same way it had at the house when Don entered it.

The pizzeria owner, who had gone across the street to see the raining in the house earlier that night, was convinced that Decker was possessed by an evil spirit. She grabbed a crucifix and pressed it against Don's flesh, which allegedly burned him and ended the trance he had been in.

When Don and the Keiffers were accused of somehow pranking everyone, Don was lifted off the floor and thrown against a wall by an invisible force.

Don allegedly began to wonder if he could control the rainfall and started to focus on doing it. When Decker went back to complete his jail sentence, he intentionally made it rain in his jail cell, baffling prison guards.

After an exorcism was performed, the alleged rain stopped, and Don Decker's life went back to the way it was before. However, he forever became known around the town as "The Stroudsburg Rain Man."

The case was featured on a number of TV shows, including *Unsolved Mysteries* in 1993. In 2011, it was also featured on *Paranormal Witness*. It's even drawn attention from New Zealand researchers in recent years.

The most baffling part of the case was that a total of nine witnesses (including four police officers, prison guards, and the prison warden, who are considered credible witnesses) have gone on record talking about what they saw.

So, what really happened to Don Decker? Is it possible that this could have been a really big hoax, including even police officers? Was Decker really possessed? Don Decker allegedly claimed that he believed his grandfather had come back to haunt him. Could this be what happened? The world may never know.

As for what happened to Decker? In 2012, he was arrested for arson when he set a restaurant in the Poconos on fire.

To date, the case of the Stroudsburg Rain Man remains one of the biggest unsolved mysteries of all-time.

The Musical Field in Upper Black Eddy

If you've ever wanted to see musical rocks, then you might want to visit Upper Black Eddy in Bucks County, Pennsylvania.

Ringing Rocks County Park draws visitors who come to hear the rocks make music. The stones in the park produce tones that sound like bells when they're struck.

It's one of the largest, if not *the* largest, field in the U.S. that contains ringing rocks, according to a geologic scientist named Helen Delano.

Back in 1890, J.J. Ott gave a concert for the Buckwampum historical society. The instrument he played? Stones that made bell-like noises when they were struck with a hammer that Ott had gotten from the then-unnamed Ringing Rocks County Park. Some have called it the United States' first rock concert.

For a long time, it was unknown why the rocks rang. Scientists discovered that the rocks ring at tones lower than the human ear can hear. It's believed that the reason they ring is due to the freeze-thaw cycle that helped form the boulder field. Still, plenty of people believe that supernatural forces are at work.

According to legends, compasses won't work in the park and animals won't go near the park. It's also said that the rocks only ring when they're in the park.

That last part *is* true, so if you're thinking about illegally taking the rocks to make your own music at home, just know that it won't work out the way you plan. The rocks lose their ability to produce music when they're removed from the other stones.

UFOs Have Been Spotted in Pennsylvania

You stand a good chance of spotting a UFO when you're in Pennsylvania. As of 2015, *ABC News* ranked Pennsylvania as the 7th state with the most reported UFO sightings. According to the National UFO Reporting Center, Pennsylvania has had a total of 3,829 sightings as of 2018.

The Kecksburg UFO Incident, which is often called "Pennsylvania's Roswell," is one of the most famous incidents involving unidentified flying objects in the state. Back in 1965, Kecksburg, PA citizens reported seeing a fireball. The fireball was seen over a total of six U.S. states, as well as Canada.

So, what exactly *was* that fireball? At the time, astronomers claimed that it was likely a meteor bolide burning up in the atmosphere. In 2005, NASA released a statement that said experts who examined fragments found in the area had determined it to be a Russian satellite but claimed their findings had been lost in the 1990s. In 2015, researchers proposed the idea that it was an Air Force spy satellite. Despite their explanations, the incident has drawn a lot of controversy and conspiracy theories, including aliens.

As of 2017, sightings have been on the rise in Philadelphia and Pennsylvania as a whole. According to a book called *UFO Sightings Desk Reference*, Philadelphia only saw eight or fewer sightings from 2001 to 2005. From 2010 to 2015, there were at least 20 sightings a year. Pennsylvania as a whole had 600 sightings between 2012 and 2014. Pittsburgh leads the state in sightings.

Bigfoot is Also Said to Call the State His Home

It might not surprise you to learn that there have been a number of alleged Bigfoot sightings in PA. After all, what better place for Bigfoot to hang out than Pennsylvania, where forest accounts for 59% of the state? People have been reporting sightings of the hairy creature for more than 150 years.

The majority of these sightings have been in Western Pennsylvania. According to the Keystone Bigfoot

Project, there have been 113 reported sightings in Westmoreland County, 43 reported sightings in Allegheny County (Pittsburgh), and 36 reported sightings in Fayette County. Chestnut Ridge, which spans from West Virginia to Fayette County, PA, is said to be a hotspot for sightings. People also report sightings of Sasquatch along the Appalachian Trail.

Pennsylvania Once Had a Witch Trial

When you think of witch trials in the colonial U.S., the Salem Witch Trials are probably the first (and maybe the only) witch trials that come to mind. But did you know that Pennsylvania had a witchcraft trial nine years prior to the trials in Salem?

In 1683, Margaret Mattson and Gethro Hendrickson, who were from Sweden and lived in Ridley Township (near today's Delaware County) were the accused. The two women appeared before a petit jury and William Penn. Lasse Cock, who was also from Sweden, acted as interpreter. Although Hendrickson's trial isn't documented, Mattson's is.

A witness named Henry Drystreet said that he'd been told 20 years earlier that Mattson was a witch and that she had "bewitched" cows. A second witness by the name of Charles Ashcom said that Mattson's daughter had sold the allegedly bewitched cows. It was claimed that the cattle provided very little milk and that some had even died due to witchcraft. Mattson was also accused of appearing in the form of dreams and visions to her neighbors.

Margaret Mattson denied the witnesses' testimony, claiming that it was hearsay. She also denied being a witch.

Governor Penn oversaw the trial in Philadelphia and allowed the jury to deliberate. They found Mattson to be guilty of having "the common fame" of a witch, but they didn't find her being guilty of using witchcraft on the animals. Mattson's husband was required to pay 100 pounds for her alleged crimes, while Hendrickson's husband had to pay 50 pounds for the charges.

The sums were to be returned if the accused acted on good behavior.

When Governor Penn asked her if rode a broomstick, Mattson claimed to be confused by the question. Penn allegedly said, "Well, I know of no law against it." Although records don't confirm if this was true or not, it's thought to be a story that was often told due to Penn's progressive views at the time.

In fact, the entire verdict in the case was considered to be a reflection of Penn's Quaker values and his overall tolerance. At the time, there were no official laws against witchcraft in Pennsylvania until 1718, after Penn had already died. (That law was later dropped in the 1750s).

According to a research at Pennsbury Manor (William Penn's former estate), the then-governor had been afraid of what might happen to Swedish and English relations if Mattson was found guilty of witchcraft. Penn never wrote about the case again.

The memory of Margaret Mattson lives on with the nickname of the "Witch of Ridley Creek."

The Legend of the Seven Gates of Hell

The Seven Gates of Hell is one of the most well-known legends in south-central Pennsylvania.

According to the legend, there was an insane asylum in Hellam Township in York, Pennsylvania. One night, the asylum burnt down. Although many of the patients died in the fire, some also escaped into the surrounding area.

Seven gates were allegedly built in an effort to trap the wandering patients. The myth says that only one of the gates is visible in the daylight, but all seven are visible at night. It's rumored that passing through all seven gates will send you directly to Hell. Rumor has it that no soul has ever passed through five of the gates and returned to tell the tale.

In case you're wondering, that insane asylum never existed, but it's still an urban legend that locals in the area like to talk about.

The Mystery of the Bedford County Gravity Hill

Just about every state has a gravity hill, and Pennsylvania is no exception!

A hill in a remote corner of Bedford County in New Paris, Pennsylvania defies gravity. On this hill, cars and balls will roll up the hill rather than down the hill as they should.

The hill has gained so much attention that it has become one of the county's biggest tourist attractions.

Although there are scientific explanations for this unusual natural phenomenon, gravity hills always draw a host of myths and legends about how they came to be.

The Siren-Like Lake Monster of Pennsylvania

Did you know that Pennsylvania is believed to be home to a lake monster? Don't be fooled, though. PA's lake monster isn't believed to look anything like the Lochness Monster.

Lake Erie, which can be accessed through Pennsylvania, is said to be home to the Storm Hag. Watch out the next time you're at the lake alone. The Storm Hag is said to be similar to a siren. She allegedly sings an enticing song that leads sailors to her, which is believed to be the reason there have been so many shipwrecks and disappearances in the Presque Isle area of the lake.

The Storm Hag is believed to have slimy green skin, venomous nails, and sharp green teeth, but it's the monster's eyes that may be the most haunting thing about her. Her cat-like eyes are said to be the last thing the monster's victims will ever see before she drags them to their death.

This Pennsylvania River May Be Full of Monsters

The Storm Hag isn't the only water monster that's said to live in Pennsylvania. There's also the Ogua, a name which was given to the monster by the Native Americans. The Ogua is believed to live in the

Monongahela River, which flows from Pittsburgh and then meets the Allegheny to form the Ohio River.

The legend of the Ogua has been around for hundreds of years. However, there have been vastly different descriptions of the supposed river monster. Some say it looks like a huge turtle, with a diameter of approximately 20 feet. Others have claimed it has the appearance of a serpent or alligator. In some accounts, the Ogua has two heads.

The one thing that's the same in all of the reported sightings of the monster? It's believed to be a highly predator monster.

According to the legends, the Ogua would lurk near the shore and wait for an innocent, unsuspecting animal or person to cross its path. The river monster would then allegedly drag its victim into the water where it would swallow it whole. In some accounts, the Ogua would use its tail which is said to be 15 feet long, to tangle its victim so that it can't free itself. The monster would then drag the victim into the water where he or she would be drowned and devoured.

It's been said that the Ogua would climb onto the shore at night, where it would go hunting for deer, which is said to be its favorite food. The beast's diet isn't limited to deer, however. It's been said that the Ogua will eat any animal that it happens to encounter.

Sightings of the Ogua started out in the 1700s and have continued to modern times. There were two sightings of the monster in 1983. A fisherman claimed to see a creature that was reddish-brown in color with a long, flat tail and razor-sharp teeth. A second fisherman saw small fish leaping from the water to get away from something. A large fin burst out of the water, which was followed by a long tail before the creature went back under the water.

Though sightings of the elusive creature are rare today, they still happen on occasion. The real question is: what *is* the Ogua?

According to some theories, the Ogua may have just been a legend that was started by parents to keep their kids out of the water. Others believe that the Ogua may be an oversized snapping turtle, catfish or crocodile.

The Ogua isn't the only creature you may encounter in the Monongahela River, either. There's believed to be a half-man, half-fish known as the "Monongy." The creature was allegedly sighted a lot by the British forces during the French and Indian War (1754-1763), even supposedly attacking them. Known as the "Gill-Men," sightings of this creature occurred frequently during the 1930s until the 1950s. Reports of the supposed monster were so common that the Pittsburgh Police launched a task force to investigate them. In 2003, a photo of one of the supposed creatures was shared online and then later removed, which ignited rumors of a cover-up.

Philadelphia's Bus to Nowhere

Most of Philadelphia's buses have a destination in mind, but according to legend, that's not true about one bus in the city.

The Bus to Nowhere is said to be a bus that only appears for those who feel truly hopeless and distraught, often suffering from pain from the worst imaginable circumstances. If you're feeling more hopeless than ever, just wait and the Bus to Nowhere will come for you (though in some versions of the legend, you're supposed to chase after it).

The passengers of the Bus to Nowhere are said to sit in silence, too plagued by their misery to interact with one another. It's said that they'll be in a daze-like state and so they ride, not knowing where the bus is going, hoping to stop feeling so hopeless. It's said that you'll only get off the bus once you stop feeling that misery.

According to legend, some of the people on the bus have been riding it for years and some will never leave. If you are lucky enough to leave, your memories of your time on the bus—whether it be minutes or years—will disappear.

So, how do you find the Bus to Nowhere? It supposedly doesn't display a destination. It doesn't have a route number and the bus's route doesn't appear on transportation routes. Some Philadelphians claim to have seen the bus, which also has the nickname of the "Wandering Bus."

This Pittsburgh House Was Once the Most Haunted House in America

The Congelier House, which is also known as The House on Ridge Avenue, was once believed to be the most haunted house in the United States. What was so creepy about it?

Charles Congelier, who was the original owner of the house in Pittsburgh, was allegedly murdered by his wife who had discovered him having an affair with the maid. Mrs. Congelier also decapitated the maid, which a few days later, she was found cradling in her lap in her rocking chair. That's enough to make any house haunted, but the story gets worse.

The next owner of the house was a doctor who was supposedly keeping a collection of women's heads in the house's basement. He was using the heads for experimentation.

The house was converted into housing for immigrant workers. The immigrants began to die of mysterious causes.

The Congelier House eventually exploded, leaving behind a crater in the ground. People who lived in the area believed that the house had been transported back to Hell.

Benjamin Franklin allegedly did some séance testing at the former haunted house.

The Devil's Road is Said to Be Haunted

Cossart Road in Chadds Ford in southeastern Pennsylvania is nicknamed "The Devil's Road." The area is so haunted that M. Night Shymalan filmed the movie *The Village* right next to it.

It's said that the trees on this road bend away from the road, as though they're horrified and trying to escape the road.

Further, into the woods, there's a stone mansion that was once owned by the Du Pont family, one of America's richest families. Known as "The Cult House," legend has it that the family inbred in that house in order to control their wealth. They supposedly secretly eliminated and hid any deformed or sickly children that came as a result of this inbreeding.

Over the years, piles of animal corpses have also been discovered in the area.

The majority of the strange activity in the area has been a result of teenagers playing pranks, however.

Thomas Jefferson's Ghost May Live Inside Philadelphia's Most Haunted House

The Baleroy Mansion is said to be the most haunted house in Philadelphia. Paranormal researchers have even called it the most haunted house in all of America.

It's believed that the mansion is home to ghosts, spirits, demons, and angels.

The house's dark past dates back to its construction. Built in 1911, the mansion was built by a carpenter who, according to local lore, allegedly killed his wife.

It was purchased by the Easby family in 1926. While the family lived in the home, they experienced paranormal activity. The family's 11-year-old young son, Steven, died in 1931 of an unknown childhood disease. His spirit is said to haunt the house. A portrait of Steven is said to have once been thrown approximately 15 feet across the room, even though the hook on the wall was perfectly intact.

It's believed that the mother, Henrietta Meade Large Easby, also haunts the Baleroy Mansion. Psychic Judith Richardson Haimes made alleged claims of communicating with Henrietta, as well as other spirits of the home.

It has also been said that the ghost of Thomas Jefferson resides inside the house. He's believed to haunt the dining room. His ghost is believed to live there because the Easby family purchased vintage furniture that was previously owned by him, including the grandfather clock in the dining room.

The Baleroy Mansion is also home to a 200-year-old chair that was once owned by Napoleon. Nicknamed the "Death Chair," it's been said that anyone who chooses to sit in the chair will die within a few weeks.

Gettysburg is Home to This Famously Haunted Hotel

As one of the biggest battlefields in the country, there's no doubt that Gettysburg is said to be the source of plenty of supernatural activity. But if you've ever wanted to spend the night in a haunted hotel, then look no further. The Gettysburg Hotel is said to be one of the most haunted hotels in Pennsylvania.

At one point, the Gettysburg Hotel was used as a hospital for wounded soldiers during the Civil War.

In the 1890s, the hotel opened the way it looks today. At that time, it was one of the most popular places to stay because it offered a number of luxury amenities, including both hot and cold water. President Eisenhower even used the hotel as a place of operations in 1955.

There are three ghosts, in particular, which are known to haunt the Gettysburg Hotel. The first is a woman whose apparition often appears dancing in the hotel's ballroom. Then there's Rachel, who was allegedly a nurse when she was alive. Rachel is known to open drawers and rummage through people's belongings. Lastly, you have the spirit of Union soldier James Culbertson, who is said to roam the hotel floors.

RANDOM FACTS

1. Legend has it that Independence Hall in Philadelphia is haunted by the spirits of Benjamin Franklin and Benedict Arnold. They apparently like to check in from time to time at the spot where they signed the Declaration of Independence and the U.S. Constitution.

2. It's said that the spirit of Benedict Arnold can also be found at the Powel House. The house, which belonged to Samuel Powel, is allegedly haunted by a number of spirits including Samuel and his wife's, who were a power couple during their time. Spirits are often said to be partying, however, which makes sense. Powel and his wife often threw expensive parties when they were alive.

3. The elusive mountain lion is believed to roam Pennsylvania, even though the U.S. Fish and Wildlife Service officially declared the Eastern mountain lion species to be extinct. Yet people throughout the state have reported seeing them, with reported sightings occurring frequently in the Poconos, Allegheny County, and York County. There's even a conspiracy theory that says that the Pennsylvania Game Commission

releases the animals into the wild to help lower the state's large deer population. These theories have been denied. Officials often claim that people mistake bobcats for mountain lions, but plenty of people disagree.

4. The Historic Hotel Bethlehem is said to be one of the most haunted hotels in Pennsylvania. Located in the Lehigh Valley, the hotel is said to be home to numerous spirits. If you stay in Room 932, legend has it that you may come across the ghost of a man who will want to know why you're sleeping in his bed. When you turn on the light, he'll disappear.

5. Charlie No-Face, who's always known as the Green Man, is one of the most popular urban legends in Pittsburgh. According to the lore, a man is often seen lurking by the roadside at night, emitting a green glowing light. He's often said to be deformed. There is *some* truth to this urban legend. From the 1920s to the 1980s, a man named Raymond Robinson, who suffered from a horrible accident that destroyed his face, used to walk at night to avoid people. However, contrary to the monstrous character portrayed in the urban legends, Robinson was actually friendly.

6. The disappearance of Cindy Song was one of the biggest missing person cases in the state. Song was a senior at Penn State University when she

disappeared in 2001. After attending a Halloween party on campus, her friends dropped her off at her apartment. A girl who fit her description had been seen being forced into a car in Philadelphia several days later, leading investigators to believe she may have been abducted by a man.

7. Irwin Road is a road in Pittsburgh's North Hills area. To locals, it's known as Blue Mist Road. This is because there's an eerie blue mist that covers the road at night. Irwin Road is said to have been a KKK meeting place and the site of lynching at one point in time. There are a number of legends about the road, including one that says a jealous husband murdered his adulterous wife and their kids and later dumped their corpses in a septic tank next to his house on the road. It's believed that their spirits haunt the road. Blue Mist Road is also said to be haunted by a deer-human hybrid and a ghost dog.

8. Between the years of 1977 and 1993, a man robbed seven banks in the Keystone State. He would enter the bank pretending to be a customer who wanted to open a business account before shooting out the security cameras, holding the bank hostage, and demanding the tellers give him all the cash in the vault. To this day, no one knows who this mystery man was.

9. The Goblin of Easton is one of the most popular urban myths in the Lehigh Valley. The myth says

that a corrupt monk in Easton, PA would hear the sins of wealthy people and then later blackmail them. The monk allegedly grew greedier over time and was eventually sentenced to hanging after he had beat an old woman to death. After he died, the man is said to have turned into a clawed goblin monster and lived in the woods. Rumor has it that he ate five of his fellow monks, leaving the monastery in shambles.

10. Washington Square in Philadelphia was used as a potter's field during the 1700s. People who couldn't afford a proper burial and the unidentified were buried in the field. Rumor has it that the spirit of a Quaker woman named patrols the park, like she did when she was alive, to protect the dead from grave robbers. The park is so famously haunted that the city's homeless don't sleep on the park's benches at night.

11. The General Wayne Inn in Merion, PA has had a number of well-known guests, including George Washington and Edgar Allan Poe. It's said that Poe's ghost may even walk the premises to this day. Rumors of the inn being haunted really began after co-owners James E. Webb and Guy Sileo had hard financial times during the 1990s. In 1996, Sileo shot and killed his business partner on the third floor of the inn. Sileo then tried to

pin the murder on his 20-year-old mistress, who later committed suicide.

12. Constitution Drive in Allentown is said to be haunted. Rumor has it that a man was struck by a train one night when he was walking his dogs on the street, severing his leg and causing him to die a slow death on the then-deserted stretch of road. People claim the road is haunted by the ghosts of the man and his dogs, with mysterious paw prints and one single footprint (from his remaining leg) appearing in the snow. Local lore also says that the nearby woods are home to tiny people with pale skin and red eyes. These rumors probably originated from a pot-bellied pig farm on the road.

13. The Wildwood Cemetery in Williamsport, PA is said to be a hotspot of paranormal activity. Legend says that the cemetery has two sides: a "good" side and a "bad" side. It's said that on a clear night, you can see fairies on the good side of the cemetery. On the bad side, however, you'll find ghoul-like creatures that are known to shriek like banshees. As you walk past tombs on the bad side of the cemetery, it's said that you'll hear banging sounds and voices. There's also said to be a statue in the cemetery that cries and changes its position at night. There's also allegedly a mausoleum that was designed by a fireman, who

is buried there with his family. The mausoleum, which opens only from the inside, is said to open at night when the family comes out to play.

14. There's a small cemetery in Catawissa, Pennsylvania that has about 24 graves. The graves have wrought iron cages that cover the burial plots. Although these cages *could* be mortsafes, which were cages that were built over grave sites during the 18th and 19th centuries to prevent the bodies from being stolen, there's another theory that's popular among the locals. They believe that the buried bodies were vampires that could have risen out of the ground.

15. Welles House in Wilkes-Barre, PA has been called "Wilkes-Barre's Amityville Horror" by the couple who investigated the real Amityville House of Horror. Welles House was built by Augustus Laning around the year 1860. Since the house was built, a number of deaths took place at the place. Augustus Laning's nephew died in a barn fire. People who have lived in the house over the years have reported strange sounds, including shrieking, moaning, banging, and scratching, as well as seeing ghostly apparitions. There have been repeated sightings of the spirit of a well-dressed man who carries a cane.

16. There have been sightings of creatures with unusually long wings throughout the state,

particularly in western and southwestern Pennsylvania. One of these reported sightings happened in Fayette County, PA in 2012 when a guy was out walking his dog and heard a "whooshing" sound. The sound was produced by an enormous, cone-shaped creature that the man estimated to be about 22 feet long with a wingspan of about 18 feet. The man described the creature as being dark auburn/brown in color with legs, a tail that was shaped like an arrowhead, and eyes that glowed a shade of orange. The creature's wings allegedly had three to four talons and it made a foghorn-like sound as it flew above the man and his dog. The man believed that the creature was a dragon. Some believe they're dragons, while others believe they're oversized birds. This sighting of these enormous winged creatures wasn't the first or the last in Pennsylvania.

17. Like just about every other state in America, Pennsylvania is home to a theater that's believed to be haunted. The Mishler Theatre in Altoona first opened in 1906. It has been said that the theater is haunted by its original owner, Isaac Mishler. He is rumored to wander the theater and leaves behind the scent of cigar smoke. The Mishler Theater is thought to be home to another ghost, too: one of the former employees' young daughter, who used to visit the theater often.

18. Pennhurst State School and Hospital in Spring City, PA was named the Eastern Pennsylvania Institution for the Feeble-Minded and Epileptic when it was originally founded. It closed in 1987 due to the hospital's lack of funding, an overabundance of patients, unsanitary conditions, and alleged abuse by staff members. Today, the former grounds are known to be a host of paranormal activity, with paranormal experts allegedly finding apparitions and voices belonging to former children and nurses.

19. The former Buck Hill Inn in Buck Hill Falls, PA was said to be one of the most haunted spots in the Poconos. The inn was featured on MTV's *Fear* in 2000. The inn was said to be the location of 73 murders and the suicide of a maid, leading to a lot of paranormal activity on the premises. Although the Buck Hill Inn was demolished in 2016, the grounds are still said to be home to ghosts.

20. The Cliveden in Germantown, Philadelphia was the site of one of the bloodiest battles in the Revolutionary War. The mansion is said to be haunted by soldiers who died during the battle.

Test Yourself – Questions

1. The Ogua are said to live in which body of water in Pennsylvania?

   a. The Delaware River
   b. The Monongahela River
   c. Lake Erie

2. "Pennsylvania's Roswell" took place in which town in Pennsylvania?

   a. Kecksburg, PA
   b. Stroudsburg, PA
   c. Bethlehem, PA

3. The two women who were put on trial for witchcraft in Pennsylvania were from which country?

   a. Sweden
   b. Switzerland
   c. Norway

4. The "Bus to Nowhere" is said to be in which of Pennsylvania's cities?

   a. Pittsburgh
   b. Allentown
   c. Philadelphia

5. Thomas Jefferson's spirit is thought to haunt which of the following?

   a. Hotel Bethlehem

   b. The Gettysburg Hotel

   c. The Baleroy Mansion

Answers

1. b.
2. a.
3. a.
4. c.
5. c.

OTHER BOOKS IN THIS SERIES

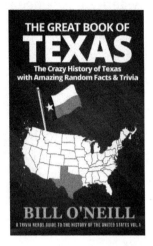

Are you looking to learn more about Texas? Sure, you've heard about the Alamo and JFK's assassination in history class, but there's so much about the Lone Star State that even natives don't know about. In this trivia book, you'll journey through Texas's history, pop culture, sports, folklore, and so much more!

In The Great Book of Texas, some of the things you will learn include:

Which Texas hero isn't even from Texas?

Why is Texas called the Lone Star State?

Which hotel in Austin is one of the most haunted hotels in the United States?

Where was Bonnie and Clyde's hideout located?

Which Tejano musician is buried in Corpus Christi?

What unsolved mysteries happened in the state?

Which Texas-born celebrity was voted "Most Handsome" in high school?

Which popular TV show star just opened a brewery in Austin?

You'll find out the answers to these questions and many other facts. Some of them will be fun, some of them will creepy, and some of them will be sad, but all of them will be fascinating! This book is jampacked with everything you could have ever wondered about Texas.

Whether you consider yourself a Texas pro or you know absolutely nothing about the state, you'll learn something new as you discover more about the state's past, present, and future. Find out about things that weren't mentioned in your history book. In fact, you might even be able to impress your history teacher with your newfound knowledge once you've finished reading! So, what are you waiting for? Dive in now to learn all there is to know about the Lone Star State!

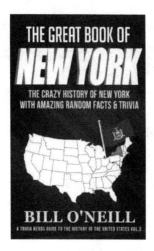

THE GREAT BOOK OF

NEW YORK

THE CRAZY HISTORY OF NEW YORK
WITH AMAZING RANDOM FACTS & TRIVIA

BILL O'NEILL

A TRIVIA NERDS GUIDE TO THE HISTORY OF THE UNITED STATES VOL.2

Want to learn more about New York? Sure, you've heard about the Statue of Liberty, but how much do you really know about the Empire State? Do you know why it's even called the Empire State? There's so much about New York that even state natives don't know. In this trivia book, you'll learn more about New York's history, pop culture, folklore, sports, and so much more!

In The Great Book of New York, you'll learn the answers to the following questions:

- Why is New York City called the Big Apple?
- What genre of music started out in New York City?
- Which late actress's life is celebrated at a festival held in her hometown every year?
- Which monster might be living in a lake in New York?

- Was there really a Staten Island bogeyman?
- Which movie is loosely based on New York in the 1800s?
- Which cult favorite cake recipe got its start in New York?
- Why do the New York Yankees have pinstripe uniforms?

These are just a few of the many facts you'll find in this book. Some of them will be fun, some of them will be sad, and some of them will be so chilling they'll give you goosebumps, but all of them will be fascinating! This book is full of everything you've ever wondered about New York.

It doesn't matter if you consider yourself a New York state expert or if you know nothing about the Empire State. You're bound to learn something new as you journey through each chapter. You'll be able to impress your friends on your next trivia night!

So, what are you waiting for? Dive in now so you can learn all there is to know about New York!

Are you interested in learning more about California? Sure, you've heard of Hollywood, but how much do you really know about the Golden State? Do you know how it got its nickname or what it was nicknamed first? There's so much to know about California that even people born in the state don't know it all. In this trivia book, you'll learn more about California's history, pop culture, folklore, sports, and so much more!

In The Great Book of California, you'll discover the answers to the following questions

- Why is California called the Golden State?
- What music genres started out in California?
- Which celebrity sex icon's death remains a mystery?
- Which serial killer once murdered in the state?
- Which childhood toy started out in California?

- Which famous fast-food chain opened its first location in the Golden State?
- Which famous athletes are from California?

These are just a few of the many facts you'll find in this book. Some of them will be entertaining, some of them will be tragic, and some of them may haunt you, but all of them will be interesting! This book is full of everything you've ever wondered about California and then some!

Whether you consider yourself a California state expert or you know nothing about the Golden State, you're bound to learn something new in each chapter. You'll be able to impress your college history professor or your friends during your next trivia night!

What are you waiting for? Get started to learn all there is to know about California!

MORE BOOKS BY BILL O'NEILL

I hope you enjoyed this book and learned something new. Please feel free to check out some of my previous books on Amazon.

CPSIA information can be obtained
at www.ICGtesting.com
Printed in the USA
FSHW021252290121
78150FS